W9-BAY-251

Connecting Boys with Books 2

Closing the Reading Gap

Michael Sullivan

AMERICAN LIBRARY ASSOCIATION
Chicago 2009

Michael Sullivan (BA in history, Harvard College, 1989; MLS, Simmons College, 1999) is the author of *Connecting Boys with Books* (American Library Association, 2003), *Fundamentals of Children's Services* (American Library Association, 2005), *Escapade Johnson and Mayhem at Mount Moosilauke* (Big Guy Books, 2006), and *Escapade Johnson and the Coffee Shop of the Living Dead* (Publishing Works, 2008). He has spoken widely on the topic of boys and reading and is an adjunct faculty member at Simmons College Graduate School of Library and Information Science in Boston and Plymouth State University in Plymouth, New Hampshire. He has been a children's librarian and library director in public libraries for more than fifteen years, most recently as director of the Weeks Public Library in Greenland, New Hampshire.

The paper used in this publication meets the minimum requirements of American National Standard for Information Sciences—Permanence of Paper for Printed Library Materials, ANSI Z39.48-1992. ∞

Library of Congress Cataloging-in-Publication Data
Sullivan, Michael, 1967 Aug. 30–
    Connecting boys with books 2 : closing the reading gap / Michael Sullivan.
        p. cm.
    Includes bibliographical references and index.
    ISBN 978-0-8389-0979-9 (alk. paper)
    1. Boys—Books and reading—United States. 2. Teenage boys—Books and reading—United States. 3. Reading—Sex differences—United States. 4. Reading promotion—United States. 5. Sex differences in education—United States. 6. Children's libraries—Activity programs—United States. 7. Young adults' libraries—Activity programs—United States. 8. School libraries—Activity programs—United States. I. Title.
    Z1039.B67S85 2009
    028.5'5083—dc22   2008034925

3980

ISBN-13: 978-0-8389-0979-9

Printed in the United States of America
13 12 11 10 09   5 4 3 2 1

To Cathie-Sue, my inspiration

Contents

Introduction

Five Years on the Front Lines

Since the publication of *Connecting Boys with Books: What Libraries Can Do* (American Library Association, 2003), I have spent a great deal of time on the road, talking to groups of teachers, school librarians, school administrators, public librarians, and parents about the special reading needs of boys. When I first started, people would show up just to argue with me. One woman stood up in the back of a lecture hall as soon as I was introduced and began yelling at the top of her lungs that I was a misogynist, that I was out to put girls in their place, and that I was making up this supposed boy crisis. She had to be led from the room before I could even begin to speak. Being a boys' reading advocate was a dangerous business back then.

In the intervening five years, I have spoken in more than half the states in the nation, addressing the national conference of the Public Library Association and more than twenty conferences of teachers or librarians, and giving more than one hundred workshops on the local or regional level on promoting reading to boys. I receive hundreds upon hundreds of e-mails from parents and educators detailing their efforts to reach boys. Much of that communication has informed what you are about to read, as have the countless hours spent talking to new friends and colleagues across the country. I have had the pleasure of addressing entire conferences dedicated to the issue of boys and reading. I have reviewed the work of individual schools as well as school districts, libraries, and library systems that have created guys' reading initiatives. All their experience stands behind what I now present to you.

Things have changed a lot in just five years. People now are not only willing to talk about boys and reading, they are eager to do so. Much of that change can be attributed to *Newsweek* magazine, which ran a cover story in January 2006 titled "The Trouble with Boys." Apparently, once *Newsweek* says something, it must be true.

In all honesty, there are several reasons why the idea of a reading gap between boys and girls has become more accepted. The writing of some great researchers whom you will meet in this book—Michael W. Smith, Jeffrey D. Wilhelm, Stephen Krashen, Michael Gurian, William Brozo, Leonard Sax, and Carla Hannaford—has gained acceptance by virtue of the quality of their work and their insights. There are also authors who not only write great books for boys but go out and speak to kids, parents, and educators about the importance of reading. Jon Scieszka, the author of the Time Warp Trio series, has been named by the Library of Congress as the first National Ambassador for Young People's Literature.[1] Gordon Korman, Todd Strasser, and other great boys' writers are being heard as well. There is also a groundswell of teachers, parents, and librarians who see boys in crisis and demand answers to the key questions: why does this crisis exist, and how do we fix it? When it is their son, their student, or their library user at risk, these people do not tend to quibble about definitions and theoretical distinctions. They want to help their boys.

There are societal factors as well, factors that are feeding this crisis, that have helped bring it to the fore. National education policy, led by the No Child Left Behind legislation, has put such a stranglehold on our classrooms that boys are falling through chasms, not cracks. The fear of draconian punishments for schools that fail to show progress is pushing schools to pressure their students, exacerbating the kind of tension that discourages boys from reading. Concerns over the impact of the media, be it television, movies, or video games, have led many to wish for a better alternative for boys. The explosion in the diagnosis of attention-deficit/hyperactivity disorder and the recognition that this apparent epidemic is hitting boys hard have also raised concerns. All of these factors and more are explored in the following pages.

Ultimately, all this recognition must translate into individual action if boys are to be helped. We must address the boys' reading problem one boy at a time. That does not mean that there are not broad, society-wide changes we can make, only that the personal approach comes first. We begin here by looking at the breadth of the problem, then turn to practical, ground-level solutions. By the end of this book, we take this all the way back and complete the circle. We begin with society's recognition of the problem, focus that recognition into individual action, then ask what we as a society can do to create a culture that supports boys' reading.

This book is the culmination of five years of research, writing, speaking, and, most of all, listening. I have listened to the stories of parents, those who have raised boys who are readers and those who have raised boys who are nonreaders. Their perspective on parenting has been invaluable to me, someone who has never raised a boy. I have listened to the teachers out there who have almost universally recognized that boys in general are in need, and that recognition of differences is the start of the solution. So many have decried the loss of control over their classrooms and expressed their concern that this loss will make it difficult to address the needs of boys. Change has never been easy in our schools; in today's standards-driven atmosphere, it is a real challenge.

I have listened to school librarians who have long recognized the importance of reading as a lifelong passion but who feel that their school libraries have been marginalized as an "extra" and their mission forfeited to a media-driven curriculum that should have complemented their work, not diluted it. I have listened to public librarians, and children's librarians especially, who have seen generation after generation of story-hour-loving boys turn into adolescents who never set foot in a library.

I myself bring to the table more than twenty years' experience, as a special needs teacher, public librarian, sports coach, chess instructor, storyteller, and program leader. When I went on the road, I found out that a great deal of my experience was reflected in the experience of so many others. The problems are largely universal; the solutions, I found, were as varied as the landscape. Out on the circuit, teaching, training, and consulting, I found my most useful experience to be that as a storyteller. I eventually came to look at ideas about how to help boys in their reading journey the way a traveling storyteller looks at stories. I would find one idea in this town and take it with me to the next. Good ideas, like good stories, are utterly unique, but they touch something universal.

Now I offer those years conversations to all. This is the result of my time on the front lines of boys' reading battles. Many of the ideas you see here are the tried and tested results of real-life experience. Like stories, the ones that fail are forgotten; the ones that succeed carry on. Let us hope that five years from now we can enjoy even more success stories.

Note

1. "Newsmaker: Jon Scieszka," *American Libraries,* May 2008, 31.

Chapter 1

A Blueprint for Boys and Reading

It may seem counterintuitive, but I begin this work on the special reading needs of boys by writing about girls and their special needs in math and science. In 2005, Lawrence Summers, then president of Harvard University, caused an uproar when he intimated that innate differences in levels of ability between men and women were at least partially to blame for the disparity between the number of men and women in top math and science faculty positions.[1] The furor over these comments was justified, for they contradicted three decades of experience in education. One of the nation's top educators should have known that differences in approach do not necessarily translate into differences in ability.

In the late 1970s through the 1990s, the "Girl Power" movement revolutionized education in the United States and reached beyond to affect every corner of our society. It was inspired by several realizations, primary of which was that girls were not succeeding in the areas of math and science, a deficit that gained popular and national attention with the American Association of University Women report *How Schools Shortchange Girls.*[2] We, at least those of us who are not presidents of Ivy League colleges, saw that it was not that girls' brains could not handle math and science, but that the way we taught these subjects did not speak to girls. For girls to succeed, we needed to pay special attention to how girls learn and to make girls see this as an area in which they could succeed.

But the acknowledgment of the math and science gap was just the beginning. We realized that the culture of our schools failed to reward the way girls relate to the world. Classroom atmospheres were competitive, active, and as such intimidating and unwelcoming to many girls.[3] Note that this is many, not all—a theme that continues throughout this discussion. While the teachers' attention was focused on the loudest and most aggressive students, many girls faded into the background and their self-esteem suffered. As Shirley P. Brown and Paula Alidia Roy report, "Researchers began to see that a more cooperative framework for learning as well as an emphasis on personal connections served girls more effectively than a competitive, impersonal environment."[4]

Finally, we realized that certain institutions and activities were effectively closed to girls, including many voluntary associations and societies, sports programs, and even college itself. In 1970, only 41 percent of college students were female, and even if a woman graduated from college she was likely to suffer from restricted opportunities when pitted against a man who had shared a table at the Rotary Club, or the golf course, with the person making a hiring decision.[5]

What did we do about these realizations? Beginning with educators and eventually reaching all of society, we addressed the problems head-on. We took steps to promote science and math to girls, changing how these were taught to better fit the way girls learn. We instituted single-gender classes, girls-only intensive classes that focused on the learning styles that tended to speak to girls. We offered scholarships to help girls who wanted to study in these fields. In all classes, we put a greater emphasis on a more inclusive atmosphere for all.

The changes were not limited to the classroom. Throughout our culture, we made an effort to make our institutions safe and supportive. The idea of male-only associations crumbled, and though they certainly still exist they are as marginalized today as they were institutional in 1970. Title IX, passed in 1972, addressed glaring inequities in scholastic and college sports, opening to young women the advantages of healthy competition and the social bonds that are formed on the sports field. Girl-centered social organizations got into the act. In the 1990s, the Girl Scouts launched their STEM program (science, technology, engineering, and math) and partnered with such companies as Lockheed Martin and Intel.[6] Perhaps the crowning achievement of the Girl Power movement is the success in opening higher education to women. By 2006, 57 percent of American college students were female.[7]

The Girl Power movement may be best remembered by the powerful writing that inspired it, and that it in turn inspired. The breadth of this writing shows the interconnectedness of the issues faced by girls—educational, social, and psychological. The trail of great books reaches back to Carol Gilligan's *In a Different Voice: Psychological Theory and Women's Development* (Harvard University Press, 1982) and stretches through Peggy Orenstein's *Schoolgirls: Young Women, Self-Esteem, and the Confidence Gap* (Doubleday, 1994), Mary Bray Pipher's *Reviving Ophelia* (Putnam, 1994), Joan Ryan's *Little Girls in Pretty Boxes: The Making and Breaking of Elite Gymnasts and Figure Skaters* (Doubleday, 1995), and possibly most powerfully Myra Sadker's *Failing at Fairness: How Our Schools Cheat Girls* (Scribner, 1994), among others.

The result of this focus and these society-wide changes was without a doubt the most positive and powerful transformation in education in the past century. We saw a great injustice, and we made basic, structural, and far-reaching changes in order to address it. We recognized that girls, on average, have different needs, strengths, and approaches to learning than boys. We adjusted our society to give girls a fair chance to succeed. We did not allow a fear of gender bias to stop us from addressing real problems.

In this brief history, we find the hope and the blueprint for addressing the reading gap that boys face today. Replace girls with boys and math and science with reading, and we face an analogous situation. Indeed, the reading gap among twelfth graders today is twice as large in favor of girls as the math gap is in favor of boys, and the gender gap in writing is six times as wide as the gender gap in math.[8] The problem is one we have faced before. We know we can fix it, we know how we can fix it, and we know we must.

NO GIRLS ALLOWED

Knowing we have a problem to fix does not mean that the task will be easily accomplished; that, too, we may learn from the Girl Power movement. Social inertia is never easy to overcome. A small example from small-town New England may illustrate this. A public library in a tiny New Hampshire town decided to make a concentrated effort at programming for boys in response to the acknowledged reading gap. Those in charge thought they needed a powerful kickoff program to raise awareness and, showing a good understanding of the issues, chose a storytelling program as that beginning. They asked me to come up and tell stories, and I was happy to oblige.

In planning the program, we made a difficult decision, and one that nobody should make lightly. We could have offered the program as one for the whole family but of special interest to boys, but we feared that this would not produce the desired atmosphere. We did not want mothers to drag in their sons, plop them down in a chair, and tell them to pay attention to something that would be good for them. Instead, we wanted to do some role modeling; we wanted fathers, uncles, grandfathers, and brothers to come in with the boys and share the experience. So we decided to make the program for guys alone.

Then we needed a name for the program, so we went back to the old television sitcoms and the ever-present tree house behind the suburban home. What was painted in big red letters on that ubiquitous hideaway? "No Girls Allowed!" That is what we named our program, thinking we were being funny. The local middle school did not agree. It refused to participate in the publicity, claiming the program was discriminatory. Then the school wrote a letter to the director of the public library insisting that the library not be involved in such a program either. And then, somehow, that letter made it into the local newspaper.

This was a small town of a few thousand people, quiet and serene. This fuss became the biggest news story of the year. There were editorials and responses, arguments in the street and the local supermarket. As I drove up that evening, I expected to have to cross a picket line in order to tell stories. There were no picketers, just eighty-five boys, fathers, grandfathers, and uncles ready to engage in a public library storytelling. That should be proof enough that attempting to ban something is the surest way to make it popular.

It was a grand night. The children's librarian who organized the event warmed up the audience with interactive games that got the crowd shouting, laughing, and jumping up and down until the bookshelves themselves were swaying. Then she announced that, since this was a program for guys alone, she was leaving the crowd to me. We told and listened to stories for more than an hour, and by the time we were done my ears were ringing as if I had been at a rock concert.

CHESS FOR GIRLS

After my overly publicized storytelling event, I began to think about our attitude toward boys, girls, and specific gender-based needs. Earlier during that school year I had offered a program at my local elementary school called "Chess for Girls" as part of their enrichment program. The reason was simple: as a chess teacher and coach, I had always had trouble convincing girls to participate. I knew that there was nothing about being a girl that made them incapable of playing chess; the problem was a combination of social factors and the way we teach chess to kids. Most chess teachers are male and teach from a male perspective, and most girls who walk into a chess program know immediately they are outnumbered and shy away.

The intention of Chess for Girls was to handpick eight girls, give them six weeks of intensive training, raise their skills, confidence, and camaraderie, and have them stand together against the boys. Chess, like reading, is too valuable to be offered to only half of our children. Did anybody have a problem with this program? Well, actually, a few boys did. They accused me of conspiring to teach the girls to beat them, which was absolutely true, but if they and their compatriots had been nicer to the girls the first time around I would not have needed to do so. Other than that, Chess for Girls went unchallenged. Nobody claimed it was discriminatory or wrote angry letters to the press. Indeed, the local Educational Partnership Council, the business booster group for the school district, gave me an award that year for innovative programming in the local public school, and the one program they mentioned by name was Chess for Girls.

What are we to make of this? On one hand we have storytelling for boys, and on the other we have chess for girls. One draws protests; the other garners awards. As a matter of fact, we talk about gender all the time. We regularly address problems through the lens of gender. It is only that we find it much easier to talk about the special needs of girls. We must get past this.

DON'T TALK TO US ABOUT BOYS

Why do we not talk about the special needs of boys, especially in education? Part of the problem is history. Efforts to fight for women's equality in our society have left us with the impression that men who fight for the rights of boys must be doing so at the expense of girls. As late as 2006, the *Washington Post* ran an article claiming that "the boy crisis . . . is largely a manufactured one, the product of a backlash against the women's movement."[9] Kathy Sanford charges that "girls are often blamed for the troubles boys experience developing literacy skills because they are said to siphon off the resources and attention that boys should have."[10] Although a few pundits on the ideological edge make such assertions, to my knowledge no serious scholarship or respectable educator has claimed this in at least the past five years.

In her feminist/queer critique of the literature of boys' illiteracies, Mollie V. Blackburn says of Michael W. Smith and Jeffrey D. Wilhelm (prominent researchers on boys and reading), "They distance themselves from the literature that blames feminism by plainly stating that they are not interested in critiquing feminism or in arguing that girls are advantaged over boys."[11] Indeed, those who are doing real work on behalf of boys should emulate this approach, and those who do blame feminism and girls' success for problems boys have should be simply ignored. To blame mainstream educators for the words of fringe elements is beyond unfair, and it does nothing to either help boys or protect girls. Although there is plenty of evidence that such backlashes exist, it is unfair to paint all or even a significant number of those who advocate for boys with this broad brush.

There is also a belief that boys have brought this crisis on themselves, choosing not to perform or deciding that studying is not as much fun as sports.

We generally accept now that gender as an influence has often been disguised as something else such as behavioral or personality issues.[12] Still, echoes of this belief remain in our attitudes toward boys' behavior in classrooms and elsewhere. As a result, efforts to address reading issues in terms of gender are often cast as efforts to lower standards and excuse laziness and uninterest. Critics have charged that the "kind of classroom that is now being described as 'boy-friendly' . . . would de-emphasize reading and verbal skills, and would rely on rote learning and discipline . . . really a remedial program in disguise."[13] This reflects the prevailing culture, one of standards where artificially defined benchmarks are used as a shortcut to serious investigation and understanding. If a segment, even a majority, of our population fails to meet these standards, then the problem must lie in the population, not in the standards. Are standards really what matter to us as a society? It appears to be so.

NATURE VERSUS NURTURE

One familiar reason not to talk about gender is the idea that gender is an entirely social construct and as such has no place in education; if boys and girls are substantially alike biologically, the argument goes, then all differences are imposed on them by a society that is gender biased. Certainly, if this were true, then any gender-based approach to education would be inherently harmful. In her article "Gendered Literacy," Kathy Sanford makes the case as strongly as any, flatly stating that "gender is a construct that shapes literacy experiences for adolescents in school."[14] She goes on to assert that children blindly accept gender roles imposed on them by adults and for evidence points to how children act in just the way adults would expect them to act based on their gender. I argue that at least some of the time boys and girls act in ways one would expect of them because they are expressing an honest, gender-specific way of seeing the world.

Of course, this premise that gender is a purely social construct is as implausible as the idea that all differences between the sexes are biologically determined. The debate should not be nature verses nurture, or even how much is nature and how much nurture. The real questions at hand are these: which factors are shaped predominantly by biology and which factors by socialization, and how can our understanding of these factors help us improve the lot of boys, and for that matter girls?

Dan Kindlon and Michael Thompson, in their powerful book *Raising Cain,* speak about the damage done by a society that imposes an artificial definition of maleness on boys that turns them away from their inner life, encourages them to suppress feelings, and leaves them unable to either understand themselves or express themselves emotionally. It is a great work on the nurture side of the boy problem. But even these authors acknowledge that nature has its place. On nature verses nurture, they write, "Clearly everything we do is influenced heavily by both." They remind us in fact that the two influences cannot wholly be separated. "It is now widely recognized that environmental factors can affect the structure of our brain."[15]

Socialization can magnify biological differences as well:

> A boy's early ease with throwing a ball or climbing may begin with developmental readiness, but his skill and interest grow when he finds encouragement for his hobby at home. A girl's greater ease with reading and language also appears to begin with an early neurological advantage, enhanced when she is encouraged in her reading habit.[16]

Clearly we must keep an eye on both nature and nurture.

Kindlon and Thompson make it clear that their book is not "an attempt to 'turn boys into girls' by helping them to become more attuned to their emotional lives. . . . both genders will be better off if boys are better understood."[17] Their example is one to aspire to. In their book, primarily about the nurture side of the argument, they carefully acknowledge the nature side as well and look for success through understanding rather than judgment. My work deals more heavily with the nature side, but it would be incomplete if it did not acknowledge that socialization is a powerful force in boys' lives and that understanding that interplay is crucial to our success.

Furthermore, the various needs of boys cannot be looked at as entirely distinct. *Raising Cain* addresses the emotional lives of boys, whereas I look at the reading lives of boys. I freely acknowledge that the presiding view of masculinity makes it difficult for many boys to connect with reading, even if they are strongly inclined to do so. Conversely, reading problems can be a major obstacle to boys enjoying rich emotional lives. Kindlon and Thompson discuss boys' need to explore and express their inner selves. I promote reading as a supportive and social activity, presenting language-related activities that foster communication, especially communication with male role models. Ultimately this book explores ways to improve boys' reading ability as well as the amount of time boys spend reading. If boys have trouble expressing themselves, that is at least partly because they lack the needed communication skills; boys who read are more likely to have at their disposal the words to express themselves.

OTHER CONSIDERATIONS

We also hesitate to focus on gender issues because other factors, such as race and socioeconomic status, seem so much worse. The influence of these societal factors is undeniable. Indeed, in the city of Boston, 104 white females graduate from high school for every 100 white males, but 139 black females graduate for every 100 black males.[18] Sixty percent of college students may be female, but there are twice as many black girls as black boys in college.[19]

In 2004, the National Assessment of Educational Progress found that the reading gender gap spans every racial and ethnic group, and boys trail girls in reading regardless of income, disability, or English-speaking ability. Twenty-three percent of white high school seniors with college-educated parents scored "below basic" in reading, as did 34 percent of Hispanic males and 44 percent of black males. In comparison, 7 percent of white females, 19 percent of Hispanic females, and 33 percent of black females scored "below basic."[20]

All this does not mean that gender is not an issue, just that factors such as race and economics exacerbate it. To be poor, black, and male means to be especially at risk. Still, without any of these other risk factors, males do not succeed at the same rate as girls. According to Jacqueline King of the American Council on Education, only 43 percent of middle-class white college students are male.[21]

EXCEPTIONS AND THE RULE

One final way in which we deny the role of gender in reading and education is negation by exception. The argument is simple: "I know boys who read." Although exceptions do not always prove a rule, neither do they disprove it. Not all boys fail at reading, and not all boys follow some script of maleness, just as girls differ one from another. That does not excuse us from looking at trends and generalities that describe large parts of our population. When we talk about the problem of boys and reading, we are talking about the boys who have trouble with reading. Not all boys struggle, but many do, and those who struggle tend to struggle for many of the same reasons. It is those boys we need to address.

Notes

1. Cheryl Fields, "Summers on Women in Science," *Change*, May/June 2005, 8.
2. American Association of University Women Education Foundation, *How Schools Shortchange Girls* (Annapolis Junction, MD: American Association of University Women, 1992), cited

in Bronwyn T. Williams, "Girl Power in a Digital World: Considering the Complexity of Gender, Literacy, and Technology," *Journal of Adolescent and Adult Literacy,* December 2006/January 2007, 301.

3. Ibid.

4. Shirley P. Brown and Paula Alidia Roy, "A Gender-Inclusive Approach to English/Language Arts Methods: Literacy with a Critical Lens," in *Gender in the Classroom: Foundations, Skills, Methods, and Strategies across the Curriculum,* ed. David Sadker and Ellen S. Silber (Mahwah, NJ: Erlbaum, 2007), 168–69.

5. National Center for Education Statistics (NCES), Institute of Educational Sciences, *Digest of Educational Statistics 2007* (Washington, DC: U.S. Department of Education, 2008), 269.

6. Lynne Shallcross, "Girl Power," *ASEE Prism,* February 2007, 31.

7. NCES, *Digest of Educational Statistics 2007,* 269.

8. James M. Royer and Rachel E. Wing, "Making Sense of Sex Differences in Reading and Math Assessment: The Practice and Engagement Hypothesis," *Issues in Education,* 2002, 77; and Michael W. Smith and Jeffrey D. Wilhelm, *Reading Don't Fix No Chevys: Literacy in the Lives of Young Men* (Portsmouth, NH: Heinemann, 2002), 1.

9. Caryl Rivers and Rosalind Chait Barnett, "The Myth of 'The Boy Crisis,'" *Washington Post,* April 9, 2006, B01.

10. Kathy Sanford, "Gendered Literacy Experiences: The Effects of Expectation and Opportunity for Boys' and Girls' Learning," *Journal of Adolescent and Adult Literacy,* December 2005/January 2006, 303.

11. Mollie V. Blackburn, "Boys and Literacies: What Difference Does Gender Make?" *Reading Research Quarterly,* April/May/June 2003, 280.

12. Kathy Sanford, Heather Blair, and Raymond Chodzinski, "A Conversation about Boys and Literacy," *Teaching and Learning,* Spring 2007, 4.

13. Rivers and Barnett, "Myth of 'The Boy Crisis,'" B01.

14. Sanford, "Gendered Literacy Experiences," 303–4.

15. Dan Kindlon and Michael Thompson, *Raising Cain: Protecting the Emotional Life of Boys* (New York: Ballantine, 2000), 12.

16. Ibid., 31.

17. Ibid., xix.

18. Rivers and Barnett, "Myth of 'The Boy Crisis,'" B01.

19. Richard Whitmire, "Boy Trouble," *New Republic,* January 23, 2006, 16; and Angela Phillips, *The Trouble with Boys* (New York: Basic Books, 1994), 18.

20. Bill Costello, "Leveraging Gender Differences to Boost Test Scores," *Principal,* January/February 2008, 50.

21. Whitmire, "Boy Trouble," 16.

Chapter 2

The Reading Gap

It is now generally accepted that, on average, boys do not read as much or as well as girls. Indeed, in U.S. Department of Education reading tests, girls scored higher than boys in reading in every year in every age category for the past thirty years.[1] Across the school-age years, boys are an average of one and a half grades behind girls in reading.[2] This disparity shows up again and again, at all levels and in all geographies. In Maryland in 2006, 72 percent of eighth-grade girls read at a proficient level or higher, to only 61 percent of boys.[3] In Canada, a 1998 study showed that among thirteen-year-olds 55 percent of girls read at an advanced level to only 33 percent of boys.[4]

What is more disturbing is that schools do not eliminate this difference; in fact, the reading gap increases through the school-age years. The U.S. Department of Education reported that in 1996 male eleventh graders scored at the same level as female eighth graders in writing and reading skills.[5] Although we have done much to eliminate the math and science gap, the reading gap remains an unresolved issue. Girls face a math gap half the size of the reading gap that boys face and a sixth the size of the writing gap.[6] As it turns out, schools are not designed to address the reading gap; much of the reason boys read behind girls is out of the schools' control, and much that is within the control of schools is not being addressed for reasons that have little to do with educational best practices.

Given that we expect schools to solve this problem, it may not be all that surprising that the problem is getting worse. The National Assessment of Educational Progress (NAEP) reported that the gap between the reading scores of fourth-grade girls and boys increased between 1998 and 2000.[7] The U.S. Department of Education reported in 2005 that the reading and writing gaps between male and female high school students widened between 1992 and 2002.[8]

Many who deny that a crisis is at hand argue that the boy problem is more about comparisons than about actual reading ability. They argue that boys are reading as well as or even a little better than they used to, but that girls are just improving more quickly and thus expanding the gap. To the extent that this is true, it is great news. Girls as a whole are reading better, which not only benefits them but raises the standard, helping all students. But that does not mean there is no reason for concern. Our society is becoming more complex; reading ability is becoming more and more necessary for us to flourish in our economy and contribute in our society. The International Reading Association posited in 1999 that "adolescents entering the adult world in the 21st century will read and write more than at any other time in history. They will need advanced levels of literacy to perform their jobs, run their households, act as citizens, and conduct their personal lives."[9] In the face of this trend, standing still in terms of literacy is actually falling behind.

This argument is mirrored by David Hefner in the journal *Black Issues in Higher Education.* Hefner argues that the slow rise in the number of black men in college is not as important as the rising difference between college attendance rates of black men and other groups, whether they be black women or men of other races.[10] The world is changing, and others are changing to meet it. Black men can lose out just by not moving forward. Hefner is right to worry about ground lost for black men in an increasingly complex world, and we are right to worry about the same on behalf of boys.

Reading skills have to improve across the board; stagnant skills are a net loss for our next generation. If girls are rising to new challenges and boys are not, is that not a reason for concern? It may be that we are seeing small improvements in absolute terms among some boys. Even so, Sara Mead, author of *The Evidence Suggests Otherwise: The Truth about Boys and Girls,* one of the strongest statements against a boys' reading crisis, must admit that "at the 12th-grade level, boys' achievement in reading does appear to have fallen during the 1990s and early 2000s."[11]

Anyone who wants a broad picture of reading success as a relative difference between girls and boys would do well to read Mead's report carefully. It gives a very different analysis than mine, but it also demonstrates the impact of point of view on the debate. Mead argues that boys score higher in some areas than girls and vice versa, so there is no reason to worry about boys and reading, even while acknowledging that boys read significantly below girls. Reading is important enough that it deserves to be looked at in its own right, and if girls are falling behind boys in other subjects, then that disparity should be addressed as well. Mead argues that boys are not in crisis because they have always read well behind girls, but the obvious conclusion should be that we just did not recognize the crisis earlier. Most frightening, she argues that the increasing disparity between older boys and older girls in reading is inconsequential because those girls' scores are falling too.[12] In my mind, that points to a growing crisis. If girls' success holds hope for boys in the future, than boys' failures can certainly lower the standards and drag down girls as well.

This disparity in reading success is not just a U.S. phenomenon. A 1998 Canadian study showed that, among thirteen-year-olds, 55 percent of girls read at an advanced level to only 33 percent of boys.[13] Professor Stephen Gorard of the University of York in England looked at reading scores from twenty-two countries with different curriculums and school formats; boys scored lower than girls in all twenty-two.[14] Girls outperformed boys in all forty countries—as diverse as Finland, the Slovak Republic, Macao, Thailand, Latvia, Korea, and Tunisia—that participated in the 2003 Programme for International Student Assessment study.[15]

WHAT ABOUT VOLUME?

Closely tied to the question of how well boys read is the question of how much boys read. A recent English study found that fifteen-year-old girls read, on a per-hour basis, almost twice as much as boys: 4.5 hours per week to the boys' 2.3 hours.[16] Just as disturbing as the difference in this study are the raw numbers. Even looking at the results for girls, 4.5 hours a week is not enough time for an adolescent to spend with text. The 2002 Sophomore Study in the United States found that high school sophomore girls read for pleasure, aside from homework, about 10 percent more than sophomore boys, as measured in time. Boys' reading amounted to 2.3 hours per week, just as in the English study. Girls were, however, reading significantly less in the United States, about 2.6 hours per week.[17]

Those numbers are most striking in comparison to a 2005 study by the Kaiser Family Foundation, which found that the average child in this country spends 6.5 hours *per day* watching television, using computers, or engaging in other electronic activities.[18] Although some of those activities, on the computer and in some video games, may include reading activities, it can be assumed that our children spend significantly more time passively watching television or playing nonverbal video games than they do reading. If boys read less than girls, and on average they do, then this is particularly bad news for them.

DOES PERCEPTION MATTER?

A significant portion of the picture involves boys' attitudes toward reading. Researchers Michael W. Smith and Jeffrey D. Wilhelm collaborated on *Reading Don't Fix No Chevys: Literacy in the Lives of Young Men* (Heinemann, 2002), a fascinating look at how boys perceive literacy and how it affects their lives. As part of his work, Smith found that more than half the boys who enter high school identify themselves as nonreaders.[19] Those who work with boys will undoubtedly object. Boys do read. They may be reading baseball cards, the box scores in the newspaper, the directions to their radio-controlled car, or the back of the cereal box, but boys do read.

I suspect that when an adult, an educator, asks boys how much they read, many boys are translating the question into, "How much of what we consider reading are you reading?" Given that context, their negative answers seem more sensible. Half the boys in the United States probably read little or nothing that the adults in their lives would consider real reading. And this deep rift in perception is amazingly broad and resilient. According to one researcher, what is surprising is "the finding that many boys who are talented readers and might not be expected to have poor attitudes toward reading do indeed report poorer attitudes and lower motivation toward reading than do girls."[20] In 1998, the University of California at Los Angeles asked incoming freshmen how many hours they spend reading for pleasure. More than a third of the young men in the survey answered "none." That is how persistent this perception problem is. Even young men who did well enough in school to get into college and were motivated enough to attend consider themselves nonreaders a third of the time. Sadly, 22 percent of the young women in the UCLA study gave the same response, indicating that a more general crisis in reading identity may be at play.[21]

Mark Bauerlein and Sandra Stotsky relate the results of a series of surveys by the National Endowment for the Arts. From 1980 to 2004, the NEA asked a cross section of children and teens how much they read for fun. The girls in the survey had always read more than the boys, but by the end of the survey that gap had grown to the point that it became "a marker of gender identity."[22] Does perception matter? Of course it does, because we will never be able to engage boys in reading while we have such divergent views of what reading is. College students must be readers—that only makes sense—but they do not always see themselves as readers. That gap must be spanned, and we cannot expect adolescent and preadolescent boys to change their worldview just to suit us. The perception gap is our problem, not theirs.

WHAT DOES READING HAVE TO DO WITH SCHOOL?

We face a crisis in attitudes toward reading among our youth. They do not feel that reading is important. Because of this attitude, many of our youth, especially boys, do not spend enough time reading, and that lack of practice is a major cause of the reading gap. Boys, on average, simply do not read as much or as well as girls. Where is that most immediately apparent? It shows up first in their success at school, where "reading ability is a major predictor of academic achievement."[23]

Sixty percent of A grades in U.S. schools go to girls. This in itself is not overly distressing, because it does not take the highest achievement in school to succeed there, in college, or in life. What is distressing is the other end of the spectrum: 70 percent of the Ds and Fs go to boys.[24] If our schools are failing girls, as the title of Myra Sadker's book *Failing at Fairness* (Scribner, 1994) posits, and boys fail at twice the rate of girls, is it possible our schools are just failing?

A 2005 Department of Education study found that boys in U.S. schools are 50 percent more likely to be held back in elementary school.[25] That same ratio is repeated in eighth grade, and 80 percent of high school dropouts are male.[26] These statistics are frightening enough, but couple them with the knowledge that 80 percent of convicted felons are high school dropouts, and you have a formula for the failure of young men.[27]

SPECIAL EDUCATION

Special education has a large gender disproportion in this country and beyond, and it has for a long time. In 1990, boys were four times more likely than girls to be in learning disability programs.[28] Combining that with the fact that 70 percent of boys in juvenile institutions have learning disabilities exposes a shadow of the correlation between high school dropouts and felony convictions.[29]

In 1994, 85 percent of special education students in the United States were male.[30] In 2001, the Mayo Clinic found that boys are two to three times more likely than girls to be diagnosed with a reading disability.[31] In 2000, the National Center for Education Statistics reported even worse findings, that boys are three to five times more likely than girls to have placements for learning or reading disabilities.[32] And those numbers reflect greater consequences elsewhere: half of the adolescents and young adults with criminal records, and half of those with a history of substance abuse, have reading problems.[33]

In 2002, a European study found that 65 percent of kindergarten students eligible for special needs instruction were male. That number rises to 70 percent in elementary school.[34] In 2000, 70 percent of children in remedial classes in the United States—across the board, in all subjects—were male.[35] What does that mean for boys in the one area where they traditionally struggle the most?

Carla Hannaford reported in her 1995 book *Smart Moves: Why Learning Is Not All in Your Head* that one out of every three boys in U.S. schools is in a remedial reading program by the time he is in the third grade.[36]

If special education is largely gendered, and attention-deficit/hyperactivity disorder (ADHD) is the primary special education issue of the day, then one might expect the confluence of these two factors to be grim. It is. Depending on which study you cite, between 80 and 95 percent of the children we diagnose with ADHD in the first through third grades are male.[37] The numbers of those so diagnosed are staggering. Ritalin prescriptions alone tripled between 1990 and 1995 and crossed the million mark by the year 2000.[38] Diagnosis rates for ADHD vary widely from state to state, from region to region, and between different socioeconomic groups, a troubling enough fact, but in the Midwest more than 28 percent of all children were diagnosed with ADHD in 2007.[39] If boys are diagnosed at a greater rate than girls, imagine how many midwestern boys carry this diagnosis.

ADHD, and its broader syndrome attention deficit disorder (ADD), is a purely symptomatic diagnosis. The American Psychiatric Association points out that "there are no laboratory tests that have been established as diagnostic in the clinical assessment of ADD."[40] If we had a purely symptomatic diagnosis for a learning disability and discovered that up to 95 percent of the children we were coding were, say, Hispanic, is it even conceivable that we would continue to diagnosis them? I believe not. We would see that the definition of the disability was discriminatory on the face of it. We would acknowledge that the issue was not one of pathology, that there was not something wrong with the individual, but that there was something occurring naturally in the population that we simply were not addressing. In the words of Dan Kindlon and Michael Thompson, "The list of symptoms of ADD or ADHD is identical to the lists of complaints most parents have about most boys at least some of the time. . . . it is evident that most of what is being called ADD today would not have been called ADD fifteen or twenty years ago and that much of it falls within the normal range of boy behavior."[41]

Yet we blithely go along coding nineteen out of twenty ADHD cases as male. We have, in effect, made being a boy a learning disability. That is not to say that ADHD does not exist, or that there are not children with serious chemical imbalances that need intervention. My point is that we are not effectively treating those suffering with real ADHD. We cannot; they are lost in a sea of boys. To some degree, the rise of ADHD diagnoses is a boon for boys, whose behavior is now not purely attributed to a lack of character. Still, to place the blame on a medical condition fails to address real environmental issues and socially unfair definitions of normality. Much of boys' behavior that we call pathological is just natural, and there is no reason we as a society have to define that behavior as wrong.

HIGHER EDUCATION

Failure at the primary and secondary levels of education does not bode well for boys' success in higher education. A 2001 University of Michigan study reported that 62.4 percent of high school girls planned to graduate from a four-year college, compared to only 51.1 percent of males.[42] That difference in expectation showed up in their preparation for college. The College Board reports that, in the year 2000, boys took 44 percent of advanced placement tests but only 36 percent of such tests in English. In another example of the reading gap surpassing the math and science gap, girls took 47 percent of advanced placement science tests and 43 percent of such tests in math.[43]

In 1996 there were 1.7 million more women than men enrolled in U.S. colleges.[44] Today these colleges are 60 percent female.[45] The National Center for Education Statistics found that, from 1999 to 2000, 51 percent more women than men earned associate degrees, 33 percent more women earned bachelor's degrees, and 38 percent more women earned master's degrees.[46] Again, we should recognize that this does not necessarily translate into fewer men going to college than once did, only to stagnant enrollment by men while women are taking greater advantage of college opportunities. We should remember, though, that a college degree today is as necessary to success as a high school diploma was a few decades ago. These discrepancies in college success point to a frightening future. If fewer and fewer men, on a relative basis, are attending and graduating from college, then there will be fewer and fewer male role models to show the next generation of boys the benefits of higher education. We could be facing a downward spiral.

MENTAL HEALTH

One final piece of bad news comes from the *Journal of Abnormal Child Psychology,* which reported in 2003 "robust links between severe, persistent reading problems and increased risk for depressed mood" in boys age seven to ten.[47] Boys are not reading well, and that is putting their mental health at risk. The symptoms have long been apparent, but now we know more about the cause.

Boys are diagnosed as mentally disturbed four times as often as girls.[48] A 2006 study reported in *Child Development* found that poor reading among boys was found to lead to antisocial behavior.[49]

Although girls are four times more likely than boys to attempt suicide, boys commit suicide at a rate four times higher than girls.[50] Girls are far more likely to attempt suicide; boys are far more likely to succeed. Even worse, the rates of depression and suicide among boys are rising.[51] What accounts for the difference? In *Real Boys,* William Pollack makes a powerful argument that many of our boys' problems stem from the fact that they do not speak, do not express themselves.[52] Pollack approaches the problem psychologically, but consider the idea that boys not only lack the opportunity to express themselves but also lack the ability. Some of the difference may be language. Girls have a much greater degree of language skill than boys do, and any good psychologist knows that the first step to recovery is communication.

We have a bleak picture of the reading life of boys, but it should be noted that the news is not all bad. Most boys do not drop out of school, go to prison, or kill themselves, and for those who do, reading problems cannot be entirely to blame. But the dire statistics reviewed in this chapter do point to a systemic problem in our society, and even boys who do not self-destruct may still be hurt—socially, psychologically, and economically—by their stunted reading abilities. Becoming better readers may not solve all of boys' troubles, but it certainly is not going to hurt, and it may save many boys from many troubles.

Notes

1. Jon Scieszka, "Guys and Reading," *Teacher Librarian,* February 2003, 17.

2. Donna Lester Taylor, "'Not Just Boring Stories': Reconsidering the Gender Gap for Boys," *Journal of Adolescent and Adult Literacy,* December/January, 2005, 292.

3. Richard Whitmire, "Boy Trouble," *New Republic,* January 23, 2006, 18.

4. Sean Fine, "Schools Told to Fix Boys' Low Grades," *Globe and Mail,* August 27, 2001, http://globeandmail.com/series/school/fix.html.

5. Lanning Taliaferro, "Education Gender Gap Leaving Boys Behind," *Journal News,* June 17, 2001, 17.

6. James M. Royer and Rachel E. Wing, "Making Sense of Sex Differences in Reading and Math Assessment: The Practice and Engagement Hypothesis," *Issues in Education,* 2002, 77; and Michael W. Smith and Jeffrey D. Wilhelm, *Reading Don't Fix No Chevys: Literacy in the Lives of Young Men* (Portsmouth, NH: Heinemann, 2002), 1.

7. Lucille Renwick, "What's the Buzz?" *Instructor,* August 2001, 8.

8. Whitmire, "Boy Trouble," 15.

9. Christina Clark and Kate Rumbold, *Reading for Pleasure: A Research Overview* (National Literacy Trust, 2006), 5.

10. David Hefner, "Where the Boys Aren't," *Black Issues in Higher Education,* June 17, 2004, 71.

11. Sara Mead, *The Evidence Suggests Otherwise: The Truth about Boys and Girls* (Washington, DC: Education Sector, 2006), 4.

12. Ibid., 6–7.

13. Fine, "Schools Told to Fix Boys' Low Grades."

14. Valerie Strauss, "Educators Differ on Why Boys Lag in Reading," *Washington Post,* March 15, 2005, A12.

15. William G. Brozo, "Gender and Reading Literacy," *Reading Today,* February/March 2005, 18.

16. Adi Bloom, "Girls Go for Little Women but Boys Prefer Lara," *Times Educational Supplement,* March 15, 2002, 18.

17. Steven J. Ingles et al., *A Profile of the American Sophomore in 2002: Initial Results from the Base Year of the Education Longitudinal Study of 2002* (Washington, DC: National Center for Education Statistics, 2005), 75.

18. Marilyn Elias, "Electronic World Swallows Up Kids' Time, Study Finds," *USA Today,* March 10, 2005, A1.

19. Patrick Jones and Dawn Cartwright Fiorelli, "Overcoming the Obstacle Course: Teenage Boys and Reading," *Teacher Librarian,* February 2003, 9.

20. Sean Cavazos-Kottke, "Five Readers Browsing: The Reading Interests of Talented Middle School Boys," *Gifted Child Quarterly,* Spring 2006, 133.

21. Christina Hoff Sommers, *The War against Boys* (New York: Simon and Schuster, 2000), 164.

22. Leonard Sax, "The Boy Problem," *School Library Journal,* September 2007, 42.

23. Randolph Mitchell, Robert M. Murphy, and Jodie M. Peters, "The Boys in Literacy Initiative: Molding Adolescent Boys into Avid Readers," *Principal,* March/April 2008, 70.

24. Michael Gurian, *Boys and Girls Learn Differently! A Guide for Teachers and Parents* (San Francisco: Jossey-Bass, 2002), 56.

25. Whitmire, "Boy Trouble," 15.

26. Gurian, *Boys and Girls Learn Differently,* 37, 57.

27. Adam Kipnis, *Angry Young Men: How Parents, Teachers and Counselors Can Help "Bad Boys" Become Good Men* (San Francisco: Jossey-Bass, 2002), 55.

28. Susan A. Vogel. "Gender Differences in Intelligence, Language, Visual-Motor Abilities, and Academic Achievement in Students with Learning Disabilities: A Review of the Literature," *Journal of Learning Disabilities,* January 1990, 44–52.

29. Kipnis, *Angry Young Men,* 55.

30. Angela Phillips, *The Trouble with Boys* (New York: Basic Books, 1994), 19.

31. Slavica K. Katusic et al., "Incidence of Reading Disability in a Population-Based Birth Cohort, 1976–1982, Rochester, Minn.," *Mayo Clinic Proceedings,* November 2001, 1081.

32. Josephine Peyton Young and William G. Brozo, "Boys Will Be Boys, or Will They? Literacy and Masculinities," *Reading Research Quarterly,* July/August/September 2001, 318.

33. Shirley P. Brown and Paula Alidia Roy, "A Gender-Inclusive Approach to English/Language Arts Methods: Literacy with a Critical Lens," in *Gender in the Classroom: Foundations, Skills, Methods, and Strategies across the Curriculum,* ed. David Sadker and Ellen S. Silber (Mahwah, NJ: Erlbaum, 2007), 169.

34. Karl J. Skarbrevik, "Gender Differences among Students Found Eligible for Special Education," *European Journal of Special Needs Education,* June 2002, 97.

35. Stan Steiner, "Where Have All the Men Gone? Male Role Models in the Reading Crisis," *PNLA Quarterly,* Summer 2000, 17.

36. Carla Hannaford, *Smart Moves: Why Learning Is Not All in Your Head* (Arlington, VA: Great Ocean Publishers, 1995), 94.

37. Gurian, *Boys and Girls Learn Differently,* 36. Six boys to every girl, reported in Matthew Clavel, "Save the Males: A Case for Making Schools Friendlier to Boys," *American Enterprise,* July/August 2005, 30.

38. Dan Kindlon and Michael Thompson, *Raising Cain: Protecting the Emotional Life of Boys* (New York: Ballantine, 2000), 44.

39. Helen Schneider, "My Child and ADHD: Chances of Being Diagnosed," *Pediatrics for Parents,* September 2007, 9.

40. Kipnis, *Angry Young Men,* 63.

41. Kindlon and Thompson, *Raising Cain,* 44.

42. Whitmire, "Boy Trouble," 16.

43. Taliaferro, "Education Gender Gap Leaving Boys Behind," 17.

44. Sommers, *War against Boys,* 30.

45. Gurian, *Boys and Girls Learn Differently,* 56.

46. "College Degree Gender Gap," *Vocational Training News,* July 18, 2002, 4.

47. Barbara Maughan, Richard Rowe, Rolf Loeber, and Magda Stouthamer-Loeber, "Reading Problems and Depressed Mood," *Journal of Abnormal Child Psychology,* April 2003, 219.

48. Michael Cart, "What about Boys?" *Booklist* 96 (January 1 and January 15, 2000): 892; and Clavel, "Save the Males," 30.

49. In the Environmental Risk Longitudinal Twin Study, quoted in Kali Trzesniewski et al., "Revisiting the Association between Reading Achievement and Antisocial Behavior: New Evidence of an Environmental Explanation from a Twin Study," *Child Development,* January/February 2006, 72.

50. Gurian, *Boys and Girls Learn Differently,* 55–56; and Cart, "What about Boys?" 892.

51. William Pollack, *Real Boys: Rescuing Our Sons from the Myths of Boyhood* (New York: Random House, 1998), xix.

52. Ibid., xxii–xxiii.

Chapter 3

Boys and Girls Are Different

When addressing audiences of librarians, teachers, school administrators, or parents, I often begin by asking them to say with me, out loud, "Boys and girls are different." It always gets a laugh. It seems so simple, so obvious. Yet in the world of education it was not always so. There was a time, in the memory of many educators working today, when to say this was anathema. We were so concerned that differences between the genders would be used to justify discrimination that we were forced to deny the apparent. The comments of Laurence Summers about the capacity of women to do math and science (see chapter 1) should be warning enough that such fears were not unfounded.

Fortunately, the atmosphere is far more open these days. Significant brain research has shown that many differences we once considered socially constructed have a basis in brain structure and development. These are differences, not for better or worse, just differences. *Scientific American* has assured us that recent significant brain research confirms that "major sex differences in function seem to lie in patterns of ability rather than in overall level of intelligence."[1] Freed now to explore gender and brain differences, and with the scientific evidence to make it happen, researchers such as Michael Gurian have made bold strides toward defining biologically based brain differences between boys and girls.

HAVE YOU SEEN A SECOND-GRADE CLASS PICTURE?

Most notable among differences between genders is that girls' brains tend to mature earlier than boys' brains. This is suggested in the earlier physical development of girls. In a second-grade class picture, it is likely that the girls will be in the back row, being taller than many of the boys. This is a physical manifestation of what is going on inside their heads. In any number of ways, a girl develops faster than a boy. By age three, the average girl is a year ahead of the average boy in language skills. Girls' brains reach their peak size at age eleven and a half, a full three years ahead of the average boy.[2] We honor that difference in brain development among three-year-olds, patiently telling parents that children will develop at their own pace and making allowances for the fact that boys often begin speaking a little later than girls. For some reason we are hesitant to acknowledge this brain development lag among ten-year-olds, despite the fact that the difference in brain development between the genders is still widening at that point in their lives.

For those who are paying close attention, there is a strong correlation between brain development and the reading gap. A three-year-old boy is about a year behind a three-year-old girl in brain development, and three years behind at age fourteen. Boys are an average of a year and a half behind girls in reading throughout their school years, starting from a small gap and increasing to a three-year gap by the eleventh grade. The reading gap can be explained largely in terms of brain development lag, making it much less frightening, because boys' brains eventually catch up, presumably along with their ability to handle language. What then becomes the issue is how we treat children while this brain lag exists, because the development lag really disappears only during the last stages of high school, and by then we have little opportunity make up for any ground lost.

BOYS ARE MORE PHYSICAL

There are structural differences between the average girl's brain and the average boy's brain, the most significant of which is the relative size of the part called the corpus callosum, a structure analogous to a bridge between the two hemispheres of the brain. The corpus callosum is responsible for cross-brain communication, allowing the two hemispheres of the brain to work together.[3] The corpus callosum is, on average, 10 percent larger in girls than it is in boys. This means that boys are more likely to work with half of their brains, leaning toward either analytical or creative approaches, whereas girls tend to approach problems holistically, using some analysis and some creativity.[4] Functional magnetic resonance imaging shows us that when boys read, the left hemisphere of the brain "lights up," whereas both hemispheres light up in girls.[5]

For much of what humans do, this is not a vital difference. We use a very small portion of our brain power for most activities. But reading—indeed, any language activity—requires the use of both hemispheres of the brain.[6] Girls, then, do have an advantage when it comes to language, to reading, and by extension to learning in a language-rich environment. This does not, however, mean that boys must suffer their disadvantage. Research shows that adding stimuli to a boy's environment can help overcome this difference by stimulating the corpus callosum and increasing the energy level in his brain. The addition of sound, color, motion, and kinetic energy (the body in motion) can stimulate boys' brains to work at a higher level in terms of language. Something as simple as introducing stress balls into the classroom has been shown to stimulate the brain. When many boys, and some girls, are given the opportunity for just a little kinetic activity, the effect is better listening skills and ease in using language.[7]

Unfortunately, the first thing we do when we expect children to learn, whether we are designing classrooms, libraries, or homework spaces in our homes, is carefully limit outside stimuli. In typical classrooms around the country, the walls are white or beige, the floors are shiny white tile, the ceilings are made of sound-deadening tiles, the windows are covered, and the desks are often attached to the chairs to create a unit that limits a child's mobility. We force children to sit for blocks of time and expect them to concentrate, then punish them when they act out physically.

To understand the effect of the basic structural difference between the average boy brain and the average girl brain, realize that a smaller corpus callosum has been identified as a difference between those people diagnosed with ADHD and those who are not, and that this difference may account for the behaviors associated with the disorder.[8] If boys' behavioral issues seem to mirror the symptoms of ADHD, remember that up to 95 percent of those diagnosed with ADHD are male.

The treatment of ADHD patients is instructive. When we recognize that a student has trouble sitting still, we do not give him a sedative to calm him down. We give him a strong stimulant to wake up the brain, recognizing that the activity we are trying to control is merely a symptom, one that can be obviated by adding energy to a brain that is falling asleep. For many boys who show similar symptoms, we can do the same thing without powerful drugs, simply by adding, or allowing for, a certain amount of stimulus in the boys' environment.

Schools, though, do not always welcome extra stimuli, especially the physicality boys often crave, and that tendency is getting worse as pressures on classrooms mount. As a case in point, the school system of Galveston, Texas, eliminated recess in order to allow more time for preparation for the state-mandated standardized tests. Schools all over the country are "cutting back on unstructured playtime for children and schools are now being built without playgrounds."[9]

A cautionary point: we must be aware of the conclusions of brain-based research on girls as well. Although the average girl does not need outside stimuli to fire the brain because of her larger corpus callosum, she has a greater capacity for sensory intake. She absorbs stimuli through her senses—hearing, vision, touch, and smell—better than boys. Girls see color better than boys.[10] Girls are six times more likely to be able to sing in tune, a tribute more to their ability to differentiate sounds than to the quality of their voices.[11] Girls absorb more stimuli, but this does not necessarily help them; all you may do for many girls by adding stimuli to their learning environment is distract them. We need to be careful to recognize and act on this gender difference as well.

BOYS SEE THE WORLD DIFFERENTLY

There are some basic psychological differences between girls and boys. Here again, we are talking about averages. Children fall along a large spectrum of behavioral patterns, and any individual child can fall anywhere on that spectrum. Still, it is instructive to look at those larger patterns to see if we can understand some of the differences in the performance of girls and boys in reading.

On the most basic level, girls tend to internalize and boys tend to externalize.[12] Girls look for the universal in themselves; boys look for themselves in the universe. Girls tend to see a wide and wonderful world and feel that everything out there has a reflection in themselves. They think, "If there is good in the world, then there must be good in me. If there is evil in the world, then there must be evil in me." This is what allows so many girls to feel empathetic pain; they feel a connectedness with the world around them.

Boys tend to see the world as a big, wide, fascinating place and feel that if they do not get out and join it the world will pass them by. They do not feel that connectedness, and they crave it. This is why so many boys are experiential learners. They need to learn by doing. Trial and error is the name of the game for so many boys, and the effect can be downright frightening.

Leonard Sax, the author of *Why Gender Matters,* concludes that boys are far more likely to engage in risky behavior and to be injured or even killed in accidents involving bicycles, firearms, or drowning. Further, this greater tendency toward risky behavior appears too early in life to be completely explained by socialization.[13] We have all seen this tendency for boys—much more often than girls—to put themselves in mortal physical, psychological, or emotional danger on a regular basis. While I was writing this very work, my teenage nephew recounted recently discovering the tractor that his father kept had separately controlled brakes for each of its back wheels. His obvious course of action was to pump the tractor to full speed, slam on the right wheel break, and send the tractor into multiple spins. He practiced these "tractor doughnuts" until the inevitable happened and the tractor flipped and sank halfway down into a pool of mud. His mother sat listening to this recounting, sadly shaking her head. Her reaction was not disbelief—for this was simply par for the course—but a complete lack of understanding.

The disconnectedness born of the typical boy's view of the world may go a long way toward explaining why so many boys engage in risky behavior. The basic idea goes like this: If you ask Johnny, he can tell you that, if someone were to take his bike to the roof of the school and ride it off, he would probably get hurt. What does Johnny then do, since you put the idea in his head? He takes his bike to the roof of the school and rides it off; the fact that *others* would get hurt is not relevant to him. The only way Johnny can know what would happen to him is to try it himself.

This difference in outlook shows up in the motivation of boys and girls. All humans, especially children, want to do good in the world. But how you do good depends on how you see the world. Girls' sense of connectedness tends to lead them to believe that the world operates on interpersonal cooperation and communication. If you want to get things done, if you want to solve problems, then you get people together, agree on the problem, make a plan, and work together to make things better. Boys, feeling no such connectedness, tend to operate on the "Home Depot" approach to life: rules and tools. Help me to understand the world around me, help me to understand why the problem exists, and show me how to manipulate things to make them better, and I am a happy man. Tools are, at their heart, devices for manipulation. A hammer manipulates a nail.

Do gender differences in outlook affect what boys read? Of course they do. Girls tend to read for clues to interpersonal relations. Boys tend to read to understand their world.[14] What is harder to grasp is that these differences affect *how* boys and girls read. Girls tend to read cooperatively, and for longer periods of time. Boys tend to read purposefully, insisting that what they read have some ultimate end. They tend to read in shorter stretches, expecting to do something with what they have read. To take it even further, do these differences affect how we promote reading to boys? Only if we want it to work. If we do not see these differences, we fail to understand why so many boys are resistant to or dismissive of the reading we want them to do.

Bruce Pirie writes in *Teenage Boys and High School English,*

> To some men, more comfortable with the literal and the explicit, it seems that both poems and women expect you to read between the lines. What teachers see as subtlety or implication sometimes gets translated in boys'

minds into a blind hunt for secret messages and the perverse notion that literature has hidden meanings. What kind of nutty person would try to hide meaning? Why can't they just come out and tell you what they mean?[15]

One final note on outlook: boys tend to be more dependent on structure in their learning styles. They more often think deductively, from the general to specific, whereas girls often think inductively, from the specific toward the general. Boys think spatially, feeling more comfortable with more space in the learning environment.[16] Boys work toward goals and outcomes, building pieces into a whole. All of this, stemming from a fundamental difference in outlook, influences the reading lives of boys.

ROLE MODELING

At one point in our history, we realized that girls were being boxed into certain roles because of a limitation in what they saw women doing. Specifically, girls saw women primarily providing health care, child care, and education. Although these were perfectly acceptable roles for girls to aspire to, we wanted them to know that there was a wider world of possibilities available to them. One of our responses to this problem was Take Your Daughter to Work Day, as it was originally called when the Ms. Foundation for Women instituted it in 1993. We now celebrate it as Take Our Daughters and Sons to Work Day, but it is important to remember its origins.

It is equally important to understand the parallel viewpoint. What do boys see? They see women doing health care, child care, and, most important, education. For many boys, their first reading teacher is female, either a mother or a child-care worker. Then they go to their public library. As a children's librarian, I witnessed firsthand the gendered structure of librarianship. At the first children's librarian conference I attended, at the first break of the day, I headed for the men's room and found a piece of notebook paper with the word "women" written on it taped to the door. That drove home the point: out of two hundred attendees at the conference, I was the only male. Do we think boys do not notice this?

As a children's librarian offering story hours to preschool children, I often ask them to draw a picture of the library, usually during National Library Week. In all my years of doing this exercise, I never had a child draw a male librarian. They would draw their library, they would draw themselves, they would usually draw a librarian, but that librarian was always female—this despite the fact that I, a male, was their librarian. Many of these children had never had a female children's librarian, but it seems that nearly all children understand, librarians are female.

When boys go to school, they find a similar situation. From kindergarten through high school in the United States, 75 percent of teachers are women. That is skewed enough, but 90 percent of elementary school teachers are women.[17] Thomas Dee's analysis of the National Education Longitudinal Survey uncovered the fact that, among 25,000 eighth graders, those students who had teachers of the same gender scored 4 percent better than average in reading. Conversely, students who had teachers of the opposite gender scored 4 percent lower than average in reading.[18] That may well be because boys score lower than girls in reading anyway, or because students who identify more closely with their teachers are more motivated, or because teachers who share a certain outlook may teach in a way that speaks to the student. In any case, it is worth considering that students read better with teachers of the same gender, and for too many boys everyone who teaches them to read is female.

The role-modeling problem goes deeper, in that so many boys do not see men read. I have for years asked audiences where the proper place is for men to read. The immediate answer I always hear is, "In the bathroom!" Yes, it is a stereotype, but the universality of the answer is enough to show that somewhere in there is a kernel of truth. Then think about where we stereotypically think of a boy reading. In the media, we see boys alone in their rooms, with the covers over their heads and a flashlight out, reading in their own little tent. When we see pictures of boys reading outdoors, they are typically in or leaning against a tree, often with a bike propped up against the trunk. The implication is clear: any self-respecting ten-year-old boy knows that the proper way to read is to put a book in your pocket, get on your bike, ride twenty miles out of town, climb a tree, and read.

It is not that men take their sons aside on their twelfth birthdays and say to them, "Son, you are a man now. If you are going to read, make sure nobody can see you." Boys in our culture just pick up this attitude through osmosis. We learn it from those around us.

A librarian in Wyoming offered the story of David, a boy who struggled to read throughout school but made it into college. On a Christmas break, he discovered his father locked away in his room, surrounded by books and reading a textbook on the Civil War. It was the first time he had ever seen his father read anything but a newspaper.[19] The story resonates because so many boys never see men read, even if the men are avid readers.

Men tend to read in isolation. John Gray, the author of *Men Are from Mars, Women Are from Venus,* calls this "cave mentality." A man's feeling of separateness leads him to carve out a place of separation when he is under stress, his cave, for some degree of stability.[20] Such a cave could be a rowboat on a lake, a woodworking shop, or a garage with an old Mustang to rebuild. Any of those choices would be fine. But too many men use reading as their cave activity. They use reading as an excuse to not be seen. That creates an unrealistic impression that they do not read at all.

If children remember seeing their fathers read, it is typically with a newspaper in his hand, either at the breakfast table or in the chair in the living room. In this case, the children did not in fact see dad reading; they saw the back of the newspaper and eight of dad's fingers. For too many men, their cave activity is reading. Sandra Lingo, librarian at Delhi Middle School in Cincinnati, Ohio, warns of the impact of this tendency. "You can buy posters that show burly football players posed with their favorite books," she wrote in 2007, "but when was the last time our students saw real live men in their homes read?"[21] For males in our society, reading is often an isolated, and an isolating, activity.

Women in our society do not tend to read in isolation; women read in book groups. Look around the country, in libraries and bookstores, and you find that the vast majority of book group members are female. That is partly explained by the fact that women read for socialization, for communication and cooperation. It also has a lot to do with how most book groups are arranged. Everybody reads the same book, that book is almost always fiction and usually a novel, and the discussion is centered largely around character development. All of these factors point to a predominantly female approach to reading.

Why should we care? Because anything we do in concert with others we do better and more consistently than if we do it alone. There is a reason we have study buddies, exercise buddies, and diet buddies. There is a reason that Alcoholics Anonymous requires participants to have a sponsor: it is simply too hard to fight addiction alone. Michael Smith and Jeffrey Wilhelm came to the conclusion, through their study of boys connecting with reading, that a social component is a necessity if boys are to engage with reading.[22]

We must convince boys that reading is a social activity, and that begins with convincing them that men, too, read. We need to challenge the men in our communities to be open about their reading, to read in public, and to share their reading with boys. We need men to be more involved in schools and libraries. As *School Library Journal* editor Brian Kenney writes, if we want boys to be readers, "we can make sure that Shaquille O'Neal on a READ poster isn't the only male reader that boys encounter."[23]

SEPARATING OUT?

The differences between boys and girls naturally leads to the question of single-gender education. Are boys and girls so different that it makes sense to teach them separately? The suggestion of male-only schools and classrooms often draws passionate opposition, but we should remember that in the 1990s schools often instituted all-female math and science classes to overcome the math and science gap. It made sense that, if girls fell behind in this area because the way the subjects were taught did not speak to girls, then a single-gender environment might allow teachers to teach in a way that did speak to girls. This same approach may be applied to boys and reading.

There is, to be sure, a long history of private and parochial schools that are entirely single gender. These schools may be the best environment for some boys, and the fact that they are voluntary means that few object to their existence. The issue becomes more clouded when put into the world of public education. Many contend that separate is inherently unequal, and the history of racial segregation in schools, from which that concept comes, should be a strong cautionary force. That does not mean, however, that aspects of gender-segregated education should not have a place in public schools. The long-term, demonstrable reading problems among so many boys prove that new approaches and different options are needed. Clearly, large numbers of boys fail to become readers under the general approach, and so boys and their parents should be able to choose options that may produce better results.

Those options should include private or parochial schools, home schooling, and, yes, single-gender education in the public schools. In this case, we are usually not looking at schools entirely segregated by gender but at individual classes aimed at specific problems. And this option is already a reality in some public schools. Twin Ridge Elementary School in Mount Airy, Maryland, had voluntary males-only reading classes for fourth and fifth graders in 2005.[24] Thornton Academy, a privately run school that operates as a public school for three towns in Maine, introduced an all-boys freshman English class to address struggling readers in 2007/8. Lyseth Elementary School in Portland, Maine, segregates two of its fourth-grade classes by gender for some subjects. Dorchester, Massachusetts, and New Haven and Hartford, Connecticut, all have single-gender classes.[25] The Walter C. Cunningham School for Excellence in Waterloo, Iowa, had three single-gender classrooms in 2006, an all-boys second grade and one third grade for each gender. There were 211 single-gender classrooms in 2006.[26] There were eleven public schools in six states entirely single gender in 2004, and

366 public schools across the country offered some form of single-sex instruction in 2008.[27]

There is some evidence that these classrooms do a good job of addressing boys' reading problems. Woodward Elementary School in DeLand, Florida, found that 37 percent of its boys in coed classes passed the state writing test, but 86 percent of those in all-boy classes passed.[28] Such classrooms give an opportunity for a very different learning experience for boys. At the public pre-kindergarten to fifth grade Cunningham School for Excellence, students in all-boy classes "are not required to sit still and be quiet. They are welcome to stand or sit or curl up under their desks, or jump up and down if they like." Their teacher reports that the boys were not only succeeding, they were thriving. Similar all-boy classes with almost unrecognizable classroom structures are reported at Hardey Prep, a parochial elementary school in Chicago, and public schools in Foley, Alabama, and Seattle, Washington.[29] Phi Beta Kappa has given at least tentative approval, saying that single-gender classrooms may particularly benefit minority and low-income students and that such classes at the high school level may reduce the dropout rate.[30]

It is worth noting that simply segregating boys is unlikely to produce much in the way of results. In Canada, "boys-only programs struggled and were terminated because the schools had not thought through why they had put them together in the first place. . . . They simply put a class full of junior high boys together, picked a few boy books, and did little else differently." Boys-only classes were seen only as balancing the girls-only math and science classes that had existed for years.[31] The goal must be to use the single-gender atmosphere to teach reading in ways that speak to boys, and to feature reading that appeals to them. It would be an equally big mistake to simply re-create a remedial class as a single-gender class. The expectation must be that all-boy classes will produce better results. Jeff Ferguson, who taught the all-boy class at the Cunningham School in Iowa, is uncompromising with his simple goal: college for every one of his boys.[32] That is the approach to take.

It is also clear that forcing boys into a gender-segregated classroom would be counterproductive. One size does not, and cannot, fit all when it comes to education. That is clear from the results we see now with boys and reading. The more options that exist for boys, the more chance there is that any given boy will find an atmosphere that fits his needs. Single-gender classrooms in public schools should always be an opt-in option.

Libraries too, both school and public, are experimenting with gender segregation for some programs. The earlier mentioned "No Girls Allowed" storytelling program in New Hampshire is not unique. The Natrona County Public Library in Casper, Wyoming, ran a series of programs in 2007 under the same name, programs that encouraged boys and the men in their lives to share books and activities.[33] Sandra Lingo, the librarian of the Delhi Middle School in Cincinnati, Ohio, ran "All Boys" book clubs for more than five years, eventually drawing in more than a third of the three hundred boys in her school.[34] The Fairbanks (Alaska) North Star Borough Public Library instituted a read-out-loud program specifically for boys in the public schools in the 2006/7 school year.[35] In these programs, as in single-gender classes in school, it is important to change the format, not just segregate the genders.

Books on Gender Difference

Brozo, William. *To Be a Boy, To Be a Reader.* International Reading Association, 2002.

Gurian, Michael. *Boys and Girls Learn Differently! A Guide for Teachers and Parents.* Jossey-Bass, 2001.

Newkirk, Thomas. *Misreading Masculinity: Boys, Literacy, and Popular Culture.* Heinemann, 2002.

Sax, Leonard. *Why Gender Matters: What Parents and Teachers Need to Know about the Emerging Science of Sex Differences.* Doubleday, 2005.

Smith, Michael W., and Jeffrey D. Wilhelm. *Reading Don't Fix No Chevys: Literacy in the Lives of Young Men.* Heinemann, 2002.

Sullivan, Michael. *Connecting Boys with Books: What Libraries Can Do.* American Library Association, 2003.

Notes

1. Doreen Kimura, "Sex Differences in the Brain," *Scientific American,* September 1992, 118.

2. Amanda Ripley, "Who Says a Woman Can't Be Einstein?" *Time,* March 7, 2005, 55.

3. Adam J. Cox, *Boys of Few Words: Raising Our Sons to Communicate and Connect* (New York: Guilford Press, 2006), 23.

4. Carla Hannaford, *Smart Moves: Why Learning Is Not All in Your Head* (Arlington, VA: Great Ocean Publishers, 1995), 80.

5. Bill Costello, "Leveraging Gender Differences to Boost Test Scores," *Principal,* January/February 2008, 50.

6. Hannaford, *Smart Moves,* 81.

7. Michael Gurian, *Boys and Girls Learn Differently! A Guide for Teachers and Parents* (San Francisco: Jossey-Bass, 2002), 56.

8. Hannaford, *Smart Moves,* 80.

9. Deborah Meier et al., *Many Children Left Behind: How the No Child Left Behind Act Is Damaging Our Children and Our Schools* (Boston: Beacon Press, 2004), 42.

10. Leonard Sax, *Why Gender Matters: What Parents and Teachers Need to Know about the Emerging Science of Sex Differences* (New York: Doubleday, 2005), 23.

11. Gurian, *Boys and Girls Learn Differently*, 30.

12. Eva M. Pomerantz, Ellen Rydell Altermatt, and Jill L. Saxon, "Making the Grade but Feeling Distressed: Gender Differences in Academic Performance and Internal Distress," *Journal of Educational Psychology*, June 2002, 396.

13. Sax, *Why Gender Matters*, 41–42.

14. Donna Lester Taylor, "'Not Just Boring Stories': Reconsidering the Gender Gap for Boys," *Journal of Adolescent and Adult Literacy*, December/January 2005, 294.

15. Bruce Pirie, *Teenage Boys and High School English* (Portsmouth, NH: Heinemann, 2002), 82.

16. Gurian, *Boys and Girls Learn Differently*, 47.

17. William G. Brozo, "Gender and Reading Literacy," *Reading Today*, February/March 2005, 18.

18. Marc Aronson, "Boys: Defective Girls," *School Library Journal*, January 2007, 32.

19. Kevin Kokur, "Turning Boys into Readers," *Casper Star Tribune*, July 31, 2007, C1.

20. John Gray, *Men Are from Mars, Women Are from Venus* (New York: HarperCollins, 1992), 31–33.

21. Sandra Lingo, "The All Guys Book Club: Where Boys Take the Risk to Read," *Library Media Connection*, April/May 2007, 26.

22. Jeffrey D. Wilhelm and Michael Smith, "Asking the Right Questions: Literate Lives of Boys," *Reading Teacher*, May 2005, 788.

23. Brian Kenney, "Is There Really a (Boy) Problem?" *School Library Journal*, September 1, 2007, 11.

24. "School Experiments with Same-Sex Reading Groups," *Curriculum Review*, April 2005, 8.

25. "Educators Keep an Eye on Boys-Only Experiment at Thornton Academy," *Associated Press*, February 10, 2008.

26. Mary Ellen Flannery, "No Girls Allowed," *NEA Today* (2006), www.nea.org/neatoday/0604/singlesex.html.

27. Liz Austin, "More U.S. Schools Segregating Sexes," *Associated Press*, August 24, 2004; and "Educators Keep an Eye on Boys-Only Experiment."

28. Flannery, "No Girls Allowed."

29. Leonard Sax, "The Boy Problem," *School Library Journal*, September 2007, 41.

30. Flannery, "No Girls Allowed."

31. Kathy Sanford, Heather Blair, and Raymond Chodzinski, "A Conversation about Boys and Literacy," *Teaching and Learning*, Spring 2007, 11.

32. Flannery, "No Girls Allowed."

33. Christine Robinson, "Boys: A Developmental Difference," *Casper Star Tribune*, August 1, 2007, A1–A5.

34. Lingo, "All Guys Book Club," 24.

35. *Guys Read Pilot Program: Final Report* (Fairbanks North Star Borough Public Library, 2007), 2.

Chapter 4

Read for Fun, Read Forever

Do not train boys to learning by force or harshness, but lead them by what amuses them, so that they may better discover the bent of their minds.

—Plato

Educators need to realize that the biggest reason boys fail at reading is that we turn reading into work. Many of us love reading and express that love to children, but it is important to remember that communication is a two-way street. It matters not only what we say but also what our listeners hear. Boys, being experiential, structured thinkers, are more likely to take their clues from what we do rather than what we say. In many ways, large and small, we tell boys that reading is a chore to be accomplished and then left behind. Here's how.

Consider what reading is to a three-year-old boy. Such a boy, if he is fortunate, will experience reading in two basic circumstances. One is the public library story hour. He will be sitting on the floor with other children his own age—ideally with an adult partner, a parent or child-care provider, right beside him. Someone will then tell him a story while showing him the pictures. Notice the distinction: the librarian is not reading him a story but telling him one. Many children make little connection between the squiggles on the page and the words that come from the reader's mouth; they have no need to. When the story is done, a child gets up, sings, dances, engages in some form of play associated with the story, maybe goes to a craft table and makes something physical, a trophy to remind him of the experience. The public library story hour is the ideal atmosphere in which a boy can encounter reading. It has all the elements a boy needs. There are abundant stimuli—sound, color, motion, and kinetic energy. The event is highly social and supportive. There is physicality and purpose. For many boys, reading never gets any better than when he is three years old and sitting at the feet of a children's librarian in story hour. It is too bad that a boy's reading life would peak at age three.

The other basic situation in which a three-year-old boy encounters reading is bedtime reading. He is lying down, with a pillow beneath his head, and an adult is sitting beside him, telling him a story and showing him the pictures. And what is the express purpose of this activity? It is to put him to sleep. If his only job is to fall asleep, this is clearly a low-stress activity. We should understand that within a few years if he falls asleep during reading time some adult will scold him. What a sad loss in the life of a boy.

Most public library children's librarians would confirm that there is little or no evidence of a gender-based reading difference among three-year-olds. Many boys attend story hour, happily participate, and love books, many stereotypically taking home piles of books on trucks and dinosaurs. Clearly, by the time boys reach adolescence, something has changed. A great deal of what has changed is how we approach reading with boys. If we only continued all the good things we do with three-year-old boys and reading, many of our problems would disappear. Sadly, we take away the supports to boys' reading one after another as boys grow through childhood. The effect is devastating.

IT'S A DIRTY ROTTEN TRICK

The bad news for boys and reading begins when we send them to school and reading becomes a "subject." That, of course, is an oversimplification. For many boys, kindergarten has been a haven, being for the most part story hour writ large. This in itself is changing as our preoccupation with standards and benchmarks has caused us to ramp up the pressure on children even at this early stage. According to Leonard Sax, kindergarten today is the first grade of thirty years ago, a time when children are expected to master basic components of literacy.

Unfortunately, "starting kids reading before they're ready can actually boomerang and turn them off to reading."[1] Sax points out that "the brain's language centers in many five-year-old boys look like the language centers of the average three-and-a-half-year-old girl. Have you ever tried to teach a three-year-old girl to read?"[2] A three-year-old girl would be learning to read voluntarily, with no pressure, no grade-level standards to reach, and no threat that her failure would cost her school autonomy under No Child Left Behind. The five-year-old boy is expected to learn to read, but under these additional pressures, with language centers like those of the three-year-old girl. It is no wonder the boys fail.

Still, all is not lost at this stage. Learning to read is still a matter of tools and components, a challenge that can still be seen as a game. It is also still a social enterprise engaged in with adults for support, at least through first and into second grade. At some point, though, somewhere around third grade, the rules change. A boy is handed a book and told to read. In his young life, he has associated reading only with a time when people read to him, and then he gets up and sings and dances and does craft activities. What a shock to be handed a book and told to sit still and read, by himself. What a greater shock to open the book and see that there are no pictures!

This is the tipping point in a boy's reading, the moment when he must become an independent reader. "Students no longer learn to read, but read to learn," as Ginny Boris, a district school superintendent from California, puts it.[3] This is also when the struts begin to be pulled out from under him. Reading may be one of the hardest skills we are asked to master in our lives, and we are supposed to do it by age seven. But the news is worse for the average boy, whose brain development is already lagging a year or more behind that of the girls in his class.

The 2007 Proficiency Assessment for Wyoming Students in Natrona County, Wyoming, reported that third-grade boys scored 16 percent lower than girls in the state reading test, which is certainly bad, but seventh-grade boys scored 45 percent lower than girls.[4] That is tragic. In Alaska, "reading scores begin dropping precipitously for boys in the 3rd, and especially the 4th grades," according to the Guys Read Pilot Program at the Fairbanks North Star Borough Library.[5] Boys at age nine scored five points lower than girls on the 2003 NAEP. By age thirteen that gap was ten points, and by age seventeen the gap was fourteen points.[6] The evidence is everywhere—third grade is when boys' reading problems kick in to high gear.

WHY JOHNNY DOESN'T READ

Reading is hard enough, but when a boy sees the girls succeeding where he fails, he is forced to make one of two statements. He must say either "I can't read" or "I don't read." Clearly the latter is the easier path. After all, everyone who has taught him to read is female, everyone he sees reading in his life is female, and a third of his male classmates are with him in remedial reading. The conclusion is simple: reading is something for girls, not for me. Here is the genesis of the tragedy that half of the boys entering high school in our country identify themselves as nonreaders. Dan Kindlon and Michael Thompson, child psychologists, report,

In therapy with boys, we frequently hear them describe themselves as losers or failures, even when they are developing skills at a pace that is normal for boys their age. Boys who struggle with genuine learning disabilities face even greater obstacles to school success, and their disheartening struggle as students easily comes to define their lives as boys.[7]

Sax writes, "If you ask a child to do something not developmentally appropriate for him, he will, No. 1, fail. No. 2, he will develop an aversion to the subject. By age 12, you will have girls who don't like science and boys who don't like reading."[8] A possible solution presents itself: we could simply start every boy a year later than every girl in kindergarten. Although not all children display the same brain lag, at least we would be working with many more kids close to the same developmental level than we are now. Some researchers assert that we could greatly diminish the number of learning disability diagnoses if we taught eight-year-old boys in the same classroom as six-year-old girls, since learning disability is largely determined as a difference between potential, as judged by IQ tests, and actual results, a formula skewed by the lag in brain development.[9]

Issues of socialization and the desire to treat children in a gender-neutral way make this idea impossible to swallow for so many people that it probably could never be widely instituted. The Ethical Culture School in New York did admit five-year-old girls and six-year-old boys into kindergarten for decades, but it was forced to abandon the practice after complaints from the parents of some younger boys who were ready to begin school.[10] Remember, these are all averages, and individuals will belie them. Still, we need to remember that even at this early age, maybe especially at this early age, differences in brain development are beginning to put boys at risk. David Trower, who runs an all-boy school in New York City, points out that "if boys need the protection of the single-sex environment at all, they need it most in elementary school because of the developmental disparity."[11] The situation only gets worse.

THE TYRANNY OF READING LEVELS

We continue to deny the existence of a brain lag throughout the school-age years. Every time we use terms like *lexile, age-appropriate development,* and *grade-level reading,* we are affirming that a ten-year-old is a ten-year-old, and that a fifth grader is a fifth grader—whatever the gender. There are, however, a myriad of factors that affect development in a child, and gender is one of the most powerful.

Grade-level reading is basically an average reading level for all people at a certain age. This means that at every grade level there are significant numbers of children who read above and below their level. If it is true that boys read, on average, about a year and a half behind girls, then grade-level reading becomes meaningless. The average girl, not the exceptional girl, in the fourth grade will be reading three-quarters of a year to a year above grade level. If you hand her the average fourth-grade-level reading book, you have just handed her a book significantly below her natural reading level. How does she react? You can expect her to find the reading easy and fun and to feel confident about her reading ability.

Now hand that same average fourth-grade book to an average—not a struggling—fourth-grade boy. He is reading three-quarters of a year to a year below reading level, and you have just handed him a book significantly above his natural reading level. Note that he is average for his age and gender, and his deficit is both natural and completely beyond his control. How does this boy react to this book that is clearly too hard for him developmentally? Most likely he concludes that he is stupid, that reading is hard work and no fun, and that he is not a reader.

Many of us would welcome a difficult book now and then. We would read it and feel good about ourselves. But what if you were forced to do something that was too hard for you, day in and day out, for twelve long years. How anxious would you be to do it voluntarily? That is the situation faced by many boys when it comes to reading. If everything you read were a chore, how much reading would you do? This is why, for so many boys in our society, high school graduation marks the point after which they never have to read again.

Of course the reason we push kids to read harder and harder material, especially those who fall behind in reading, is to make them better readers. It seems logical that reading harder material will make you a better reader. But research does not support this view. Stephen Krashen, in his groundbreaking *The Power of Reading,* makes a dramatic argument that the acquisition of language skills such as vocabulary, structure, and grammar has little or nothing to do with the complexity of one's reading and everything to do with volume.[12] The key to becoming a better reader lies not in your level of reading but in how much you read.

Indeed, research indicates that "reading amount and reading achievement are . . . reciprocally related. . . . as reading amount increases, reading achievement increases, which in turn increases reading amount."[13] On that basis, pushing children to read harder materials is probably counterproductive. Children naturally spend more time reading things that are fun and easy, and things they choose themselves, than they do reading things that are difficult and forced upon them.

READING IN VOLUME

If volume is what matters, then our focus should be on encouraging kids to read for pleasure rather than on assigning them reading that we perceive to be good for them. The Organisation for Economic Co-operation and Development found that pleasure reading is more important to academic success than even socioeconomic status.[14] Krashen determined that "light reading can serve as a conduit to heavier reading: it provides both the motivation for more reading and the linguistic competence that makes harder reading possible."[15] In a study of high-achieving middle school boys, Sean Cavazos-Kottke found that even "talented readers can make profound personal connections to (and between) texts that teachers might be inclined to dismiss as 'light' reading, indicating a more complex orientation toward reading materials than might be apparent on the surface."[16]

The answer, then, is to allow children to choose their own level of reading whenever possible, and to the greatest extent possible. This is not easy to do, especially for teachers, parents, and librarians who worry that a child is falling behind. But it is then, especially, that we need to make that leap of faith. Such a child is bound to perceive the tension that adults feel about him and reading, and such tension will not help his confidence or motivation. The leap of faith is easier to make after one has read and internalized Krashen's research.

And don't forget that choice in reading level has two sides. If it is true that time spent with text is the most important factor in the development of reading, then we should not restrict a child to reading below a certain level any more than we should restrict him to reading above a certain level. Too often in my career I have seen an adult take a book out of an excited boy's hands, claiming that it is too hard a read for him. Some researchers noting this circumstance of children choosing books apparently far above their capacity have found that interest level overcame such difficulties to a surprising degree.[17]

The fear is that a boy will spend two weeks struggling with too hard a book, get discouraged, and put it down unfinished. But I suggest that there is nothing wrong with this. When the child is no longer getting any meaning out of the struggle, he will stop struggling. Until then, he is spending time with text, which should be our goal. Every home, library, and classroom in the country should display this poster: "Children do not read to their reading level. Children read to their interest level." It would be a good daily reminder to all of us adults who worry about the struggling child readers in our lives.

HOW TO READ VERSUS WHY TO READ

How do we react when boys, or girls for that matter, fall behind in reading? The research suggests that we put them in a corner, surrounded by piles of high-interest reading materials at various levels, and tell them they can read until they catch up to the rest of the class. But we do not do that. Instead, we place such children in some form of remedial reading class and proceed to give them intensive instruction in reading. We break down language into its component parts. We focus on hard, practical skills training in the fundamentals of phonics and structure. We take away the books and hand them flash cards and worksheets instead.[18]

The point is to build up weaknesses in the literacy of the students, and to raise their confidence as well. The theory is good for boys, who may be more able to identify with the mechanical aspects of reading than with the make-believe world of fiction. As far as those efforts go, remedial reading is valuable, but we have to remember that skills and confidence produce only the possibility of reading success. Ultimately it is practice that makes good readers. Julie Dahlhauser, one of our nation's most insightful school librarians, sums up the issue as well as anyone: "The classroom teachers are already teaching them how to read; it is my job to teach them why to read."[19]

Too often, when boys fall behind in reading, remediation becomes the focus. At worst, boys are taken out of regular reading classes in order to receive more structured reading instruction. Although well intentioned, this approach simply does not work. Language is too complex for anyone to absorb enough of it piecemeal to gain proficiency. Consider the single issue of vocabulary. The low end of estimates of the standard adult vocabulary is forty thousand words.[20] Consider the consequences if it takes even a quarter of that to read an adult newspaper. If a child is given ten vocabulary words a week to memorize, for forty weeks a year during school, he will need twenty-five years of schooling to read the average newspaper. Obviously, we are not willing to wait that long.

Study after study bears out this conclusion: structured language instruction does not produce readers. Most of the studies that Krashen found reported no effect on spelling progress when teachers simply stopped teaching spelling. Vocabulary instruction was found to do little more than provide students with synonyms for words, not effective definitions. In all cases, student-driven free reading produced as good or better results than language instruction.[21]

Apply this same reasoning, and it is clear that children learn much more grammar, usage, and sentence structure by reading than they can ever learn in language arts classes. Reading comprehension exercises are a staple of structured language instruction, often defended as feeding boys' natural curiosity and love for nonfiction. But these exercises do not, in fact, appeal to boys' preference for informational reading. According to Donna Lester Taylor, "Reading for inquiry is different than reading for comprehension. . . . it goes further to deepen understanding and make sense of the world."[22] Simply put, reading something just to answer a few questions often seems pointless to many boys, especially those already struggling with language.

Instruction may be necessary to teach someone how to read, but it will never create readers. Only reading can do that, and that means that those who are fortunate enough to be born into a situation where reading as an independent activity is honored are at a vast advantage over those who are not. As Krashen puts it, "Traditional language arts instruction . . . is merely a test, a test that privileged children, who grow up with books, pass and that less fortunate children fail. . . . and like victims of child abuse, they blame themselves."[23]

THE CULTURE OF STANDARDS

Unfortunately, our society has abandoned any commitment to literacy in favor of a commitment to standards. Standards are arbitrary, artificially set, unconnected to real success because they require quantification. Because they cannot allow for differences in development, they are unfair even when evenly applied. The headlong rush to apply standards at the federal or state level has diverted classroom time, teachers' energy, and scarce resources from the creation of readers to the creation of test takers. The standardized testing alone required for No Child Left Behind is estimated to have cost $5.3 billion between 2002 and 2008.[24] Might that money have been better spent on books to put in our classrooms and school libraries? England at least made a small attempt to follow this path in 2007 when its secretary for Education and Skills enacted a program costing £600,000 that offered all high schools a chance to choose twenty books for their school libraries from a national list of boy-friendly titles.[25]

This culture of standards in the United States has fueled the explosion of "reading management programs" such as the popular Accelerated Reader program. Their promise is to promote reading by way of our obsession with standards. They aim to promote reading in volume, then quantify the success of that reading. It is an admirable goal, but these programs have by and large failed miserably. A standard feature of many of these programs is a list of books for students to choose from, acknowledging the role of choice in self-directed reading. Unfortunately, the lists, no matter how long, are by their very nature circumscribed. They are built on the same assumptions that inform curriculum development and so suffer the same limitations: a skewing toward older books, fiction, and character-heavy works over plot-based works. I have yet to see a list that comes close to honoring the rightful place of nonfiction.

Many programs are designed to honor all reading at all levels, assigning points for certain reading levels. To accumulate 10 points, a student can read either two 5.0-point books or four 2.5-point books. But many schools choose not to take advantage of this feature, instead requiring students to read books with points equivalent to their grade level and thereby perpetuating the same bias toward harder reading that has always victimized the struggling boy reader. Beyond that, point systems shift the focus from the reading to the assessment, perpetuating the culture of standards. Librarians around the country bemoan the exchange with a reader in one of these point-based systems:

> Reader: "I need to find a book."
> Librarian: "What kind of book would you like?"
> Reader: "I want a four point two."
> Librarian: "Yes, but what kind of book do you enjoy?"
> Reader: "I would enjoy a book that is a four point two."
> Librarian: "All right, what was the last book you enjoyed?"
> Reader: "A four point one."

Krashen's research found no evidence that reading management programs improved reading achievement or attitudes about reading.[26] Once again, the resources we put into purchasing and administering such programs would probably be better spent on books.

The disaster goes deeper than the squandering of resources. The obsession with some artificial definition of accountability has created a culture of standards. Culture is a reflection of values—so what do our children learn about our values? Where do we focus our attention? What makes us passionate? It is not reading, certainly; it is the ability to answer disconnected questions with objective accuracy under artificial time pressure. What chance is there that such a culture will inspire learners? Alison Follos, school librarian at an alternative school in Vermont and author of *Reviving Reading: School Library Programming, Author Visits and Books That Rock!* observes that "teaching to increase state standards and national achievement scores frustrates teachers, fails students, and places erroneous and erratic pressures on education. When school systems use a generic prescription to suit all students across the board, individual learning styles are cheated and creativity is stifled."[27] Other researchers have noted that "the lack of boys' success in formal schooling activities . . . can . . . be framed as resistance, both conscious and unconscious, against meaningless, mindless, boring schooling or workplace activities and assignments."[28]

EXPOSE BOYS TO STORY

So what, ultimately, is lost when we focus on worksheets and filling in bubbles on a test sheet, rather than on reading? The flow, the narrative, the joy, the story—that is what is lost. Many boys who fall behind in reading as early as the third grade are denied the one thing that would allow them to catch up. While they struggle to fill out worksheets, their classmates are reading. We need to give all the good parts of reading back to boys. We need to expose them to story.

Story is the structure of life. We sometimes believe that structure comes naturally to children, but it is learned throughout life—and for the young, story is the vehicle that delivers the concepts of structure. Story teaches us chronology, logical progression, cause and effect, and the other ways that A leads to B leads to C. Boys who are not exposed to story fail to internalize these concepts, and, when more complex structure is presented to them in the form of more complex reading, they are even less able to comprehend it. We desperately need to expose boys, especially those boys who struggle to read, to vast amounts of story. The more they fall behind, the more story they need.

Books about Reading and Learning

Hannaford, Carla. *Smart Moves: Why Reading Is Not All in Your Head.* Great River Books, 1995.

Krashen, Stephen. *The Power of Reading: Insights from the Research.* 2nd ed. Libraries Unlimited, 2004.

Notes

1. Leonard Sax, *Why Gender Matters: What Parents and Teachers Need to Know about the Emerging Science of Sex Differences* (New York: Doubleday, 2005), 94–95.

2. Leonard Sax, "The Boy Problem," *School Library Journal,* September 2007, 43.

3. Gabriel Alexander, "CUSD Looks to Close Reading, Math Gap between Boys, Girls," *Clovis Independent,* June 9, 2006, 1.

4. Christine Robinson, "Boys: A Developmental Difference," *Casper Star Tribune,* August 1, 2007, A5.

5. *Guys Read Pilot Program: Final Report* (Fairbanks North Star Borough Public Library, 2007), 1.

6. Bill Costello, "Leveraging Gender Differences to Boost Test Scores," *Principal,* January/February 2008, 50.

7. Dan Kindlon and Michael Thompson, *Raising Cain: Protecting the Emotional Life of Boys* (New York: Ballantine, 2000), 33.

8. Amanda Ripley, "Who Says a Woman Can't Be Einstein?" *Time,* March 7, 2005, 56.

9. Kindlon and Thompson, *Raising Cain,* 32–33.

10. Ibid., 33.

11. Ibid., 24.

12. Stephen Krashen, *The Power of Reading* (Westport, CT: Libraries Unlimited, 2004), 116.

13. Christina Clark and Kate Rumbold, *Reading for Pleasure: A Research Overview* (National Literacy Trust, 2006), 9.

14. Ibid., 6.

15. Krashen, *Power of Reading,* 116.

16. Sean Cavazos-Kottke, "Five Readers Browsing: The Reading Interests of Talented Middle School Boys," *Gifted Child Quarterly,* Spring 2006, 132.

17. Clark and Rumbold, *Reading for Pleasure,* 21.

18. William G. Brozo, "Bridges to Literacy for Boys," *Educational Leadership,* September 2006, 71.

19. Julie Dahlhauser, "Motivating Boys as Beginning Readers," *Teacher Librarian,* February 2003, 29.

20. Krashen, *Power of Reading,* 18–19.

21. Ibid., 19–25.

22. Donna Lester Taylor, "'Not Just Boring Stories': Reconsidering the Gender Gap for Boys," *Journal of Adolescent and Adult Literacy,* December/January 2005, 297.

23. Krashen, *Power of Reading,* 38.

24. Ibid., 77.

25. "Secondary Schools Get Free Books to Boost Reading among Teenage Boys," *M2Press-WIRE,* May 16, 2007.

26. Krashen, *Power of Reading,* 119.

27. Alison M. G. Follos, *Reviving Reading: School Library Programming, Author Visits and Books That Rock!* (Westport, CT: Libraries Unlimited, 2006), 14.

28. Kathy Sanford, Heather Blair, and Raymond Chodzinski, "A Conversation about Boys and Literacy," *Teaching and Learning,* Spring 2007, 9.

Chapter 5

Exposing Boys to Story

*Fiction is, after all, only a means of
transport. Story offers more: the goods.
Story is the freight that fiction, at its best,
delivers. Story has shape, weight, and
consequence. Story matters.*
— Tim Wynne-Jones

READING OUT LOUD

When we set out to expose boys to story, the easiest and most powerful method is to read out loud to them. I often tell parents, teachers, and librarians that they can stop reading to boys when the boys turn ninety years old and can no longer hear. Until then, reading out loud to boys is a must.

I can clearly remember my elementary school days, when my third-grade teacher would read to the class for the last hour of every Friday. One of the reasons I can remember that so clearly is that she chose to read to us the Little House on the Prairie series by Laura Ingalls Wilder, a series that held no fascination for me, an eight-year-old boy. Still, it was the most positive memory I carry from that year. Reading out loud to children is so powerful that she could have read the technical specifications for a washing machine and I would have enjoyed the experience. It was also an extremely effective means of classroom control, because nobody wanted to endanger reading time by misbehaving. Thursdays became the scholastic equivalent of the week before Christmas. Not hearing teacher read out loud was analogous to getting coal in your stocking.

Reading out loud has several beneficial effects. The powerful boost to boys' perception of reading is just the beginning; it harkens back to story hour, which for many boys was the last time they enjoyed reading. I have personally heard children who read poorly or not at all say that they do not want to learn how to read because, if they do, adults will stop reading to them. Sadly, their fears are well founded. I have also heard teachers tell parents of third graders to stop reading to their children; their children now know how to read and should be reading to the parents. We must come to understand that, for a child who loves the low-pressure, stimulus-rich, highly social activity of listening to someone read out loud, this amounts to punishing the child for learning how to read.

Reading out loud to children also exposes them to stories they might miss on their own. Reading is a cumulative endeavor, with newer and more advanced works building on earlier ones. The less boys read over time, the more difficult it is for them to enter the world of reading later on. Reading out loud to boys sparks brain activity by offering auditory stimuli. The best news is that, according to Stephen Krashen's research, hearing stories read out loud has much the same language attainment effect as reading itself.[1] Listening to complex language read out loud improves vocabulary, grammar, and sentence and story structure awareness. It does not do much to improve spelling, but beyond that, listening to stories read out loud can make boys better readers.

The bad news is that reading out loud is not a significant part of most children's lives. It starts at home. An English study found that only 53 percent of parents of children up to four years old read every day or night to their children. That is a frightening thought, but for parents of children ages nine to twelve, that number drops to 21 percent.[2] In schools, time pressure on teachers, caused by the demands of standardized testing, health initiatives, and the myriad of other programs that impinge on the classroom, makes curriculum time short. Add to that the idea that many teachers do not realize the benefits of reading out loud or are distracted by the outside pressures they feel, and you create the feeling among many teachers that they either do not have time to read out loud or have better things to do with their classroom time. One teacher told me that if her principal caught her "just reading" to her class he would fire her.

There is no doubt that teachers do not have significant classroom time to read to children. We should certainly work to remedy that. Most classrooms would be far more effective if teachers had more control of their time, and if they chose to use that time to expose kids to more books than the children would probably encounter on their own. Barring that advancement, we are faced with a problem: how to get more reading into boys' days when there is no classroom time to do it. The answer is simple. We need to read to boys during nonclassroom, noncurriculum times.

LITERARY LUNCH

In Greenland, New Hampshire, the public library and school combined to create a noncurriculum reading time program, one that every school in this country could, and probably should, institute in some form. The motivation for the program is important. The Children's Librarians of New Hampshire sponsors an annual readers' choice award for the favorite children's book of the year, called the Great Stone Face Award. The award is voted on by the children of New Hampshire themselves. A committee of librarians chooses a list of twenty-five books that are set before fourth-, fifth-, and sixth-grade students in schools and libraries in September. In the contest's early years, children were asked to read at least seven of the books on the list, and then in April they could vote for their favorite books.

Although this type of program goes a long way to honoring the types of reading that speak to children and encourages self-directed reading, there were problems. The list itself was a limitation, more so because of the absolutely natural narrowness of viewpoint represented by the choosing committee. They were all librarians, with a relatively narrow definition of what constitutes a "good book." Like most awards chosen by educators for children, the list was heavily geared toward fiction, and specifically novels. Most of the committee members, year in and year out, were female, reflecting the gender imbalance within the profession. It is natural that they would choose books that spoke to them, and the number of books on the list with real guy appeal was small.

In addition, the list was tied to reading level, that artificial average that denies the existence of a brain development lag for boys. Books were chosen from the fourth- to sixth-grade reading level. Also, the natural preference of librarians for more complex reading meant that the list was skewed upward even within these bounds. Boys, who read on average a year and a half behind girls of the same age, often found little on the list that would not be a struggle. Indeed, the average fourth-grade boy would find nothing within his natural reading level.

Add to these challenges the requirement of reading seven books in seven months, in addition to their curriculum reading, and you have a burden too great. For too many boys the challenge was impossible, and so with no prospect of reading the required seven books they simply did not participate at all. They were effectively disenfranchised, and the level of participation by boys made this all too clear. We simply had to unstack the deck.

Largely to address this problem, the public library and the school teamed up to present a program called "Literary Lunch." It was brilliant in its simplicity. Public librarians went into the school at the beginning of the school year and booktalked, or gave short commercials for, every book on the Great Stone Face list of nominees. These booktalks were made to every fourth, fifth, and sixth grader. That done, the school librarian produced sign-up sheets that listed the title of one of the books on the list, a range of dates (a week at a time), and the name of a reader. Students would sign up for a literary lunch that interested them.

When the first day of their literary lunch arrived, the students who signed up were allowed to cut to the front of the lunch line, a small but surprisingly popular part of the logistics of the program. They then took their lunch out of the chaos of the school cafeteria and into an empty classroom. Twenty-five students could sit at the classroom desks and eat their lunch while an adult read them the book.

Amazingly, that really was the extent of the program. The reader simply read until the bell rang and put a bookmark in the book. The next day, he or she started up again. The goal was to finish the book sometime around the end of lunch on Friday, which was easy enough with a little planning. All the reader had to do was divide the number of pages in the book by five, mark the needed daily endpoints, each day read to that point, then either open a discussion if there was time left over or speed-read if time was short. Students, of course, were more than amused to hear how fast I could read under time pressure.

The program was so simple, and the students so jaded by our culture of standards, that when first presented with the program many would not believe. Inevitably, they asked some version of the question, "What's the catch?" "Are we being tested on this?" It is our own fault; adults have taught our students that anything worth teaching is worth testing. No, we replied, there will be no test. "Will we have to write a book report?" many would ask. Again, it is our own fault. We have convinced our students that reading is a chore. If it does not involve work, then it is not really reading. No, we would assure them, no book reports. They asked if they were getting credit, if they would have to read out loud, and any number of other questions, unbelieving that any adult would take that much time out of their day to simply read to them.

My favorite way of defusing these fears was to inform the students on the first day of the program that if they got tired during the reading they were allowed to put their heads down and take a nap. I assured them that we would catch them up on the story before the beginning of the next day's reading. What we had done in effect was revive bedtime reading for upper elementary students, harkening back to a time when most of them enjoyed reading for the pure pleasure of it. Their reaction was beyond heartening. We were unable to keep up with the demand. Many students signed up for six, seven, or more literary lunches. We would get everyone into one, then try to get those who wanted it into more. We could never seem to create enough spots for any child to have any more than three literary lunches in a year.

The great result of this program, beyond simply exposing a large number of students to some great stories, was to reenfranchise many boys in the Great Stone Face Award voting. Seven books in seven months may have seemed impossible to many boys, but if they heard two or three of the books on the list read out loud, then the challenge was down to four or five. Once it seemed possible, boys were far more likely to try. And we found another way to put the goal within reach of all children: audiobooks—but more on that later.

How do you make literary lunch happen? Ideally, this is a time for school librarians to step up and prove their place as experts on, and advocates of, reading. The school librarian is the natural person to administer the program, securing classroom space, signing up readers, and publicizing the program. Reading specialists traditionally take the lead in promoting the skills involved in reading, but it is the school librarian who should be on the vanguard of promoting reading as a lifelong activity. Of course, reading specialists are more effective when they dedicate themselves to spreading both the skills and the love of reading, and so they should embrace literary-lunch-type programs as well.

Who do you recruit for readers? The first targets should be public librarians, who not only need the contact with the masses of children available through schools but also read out loud to children for a living. Public librarians are most likely to read in a way that engages the listeners and convinces them that reading is fun and enjoyable.

After public librarians, the next readers should be from the school's administration. Boys are structured thinkers, meaning that they depend more on a person's actions than on their words. It is pointless for a principal to tell his or her students that reading is important if the students never see the principal read. It may actually be counterproductive, giving the more jaded students the impression that educators are hypocrites. Every member of the school's administration, from the principal down, needs to take a turn at literary lunch.

Next, every male adult in the building should be tapped. This is basic role modeling. Only 10 percent of elementary school teachers are male; we must use them to the greatest advantage. This includes teachers, specialists, even custodians.

Custodians have been among the best readers at such programs, in my experience and in reports from others who have replicated the program. Custodians are often among the most popular people in any school, for the simple reason that they are the only adults who never give the students any work. Many school custodians are school custodians because they like kids; they could, after all, work anywhere, including locked office buildings where they would be likely to encounter much less vomit. Use their enthusiasm. Many may feel self-conscious about their reading ability, but that can be easily overcome with one or two short training sessions.

Then, simply open up the literary lunch program to any member of the faculty who wants to participate. Many teachers would dearly like to read to children in their classrooms if they only had the time. Then go out into the community. Again, this is a good time to look for male readers. It is important to list the readers when signing up students, since many boys will trust a male reader to at least choose books that might appeal to them. Go after police officers, firefighters, businesspeople, and politicians. One school librarian described her recruiting efforts to me: "I have snared all the males who have made the mistake of being in eyeshot. I have dads, firemen, maintenance guys, male teachers, husbands of teachers, and retired male teachers all lined up, and I am going to hit the post office and the police station to see if I can get some volunteers. No one is safe." Politicians usually like to spend the last few weeks before an election being highly visible while not saying anything self-destructive. What better opportunity than to be seen, reported on, and photographed reading to children?

TAKING IT FURTHER

Once you accept the general concept of reading outside curriculum time, the possibilities are endless. Literary lunch has been replicated across the country in hundreds of incarnations. The boys at an Albany, New York, middle school christened their program "Read and Feed." The Fairbanks North Star Borough Public Library in Fairbanks, Alaska, organized the "Guys Read" program, a form of literary lunch for fourth-grade boys in three elementary schools. The library put together two-man teams of readers and armed them, not only with books to read, but with flash drives loaded with images from each of the books. At each reading there was a laptop computer and a media projector. The images from the books were projected onto a screen so that the boys could follow the pictures as well as the words. This added visual as well as audio stimuli, and the team approach to reading added even more role modeling. The public library donated three copies of each of the seven books used to each of the schools involved.[3]

The Fairbanks pilot program's final report claimed, "The boys' butts were planted in their chairs, their mouths were full, their hands were occupied, and their eyes and minds were engaged." The first year of the program was so successful that three copies of each book was not enough to fill the demand, and it was suggested that five copies be provided in the second year. In all the meetings in all the schools, only two disruptions were reported, neither requiring the boy to leave the room.[4]

Lisa Casey, the librarian at the Jamestown (Rhode Island) School District, made literary lunch a weekly event and found readers who could bring some demonstration or activity to the reading. One read *Houdini: The World's Greatest Mystery Man and Escape King* by Kathleen Krull (Walker Books for Young Readers, 2005) and taught the kids a trick with rubber bands that made them look like they lost a finger. Another read *My Life in Dog Years* by Gary Paulsen (Yearling, 1999) and accompanied the story with pelts and skeletons for the children to handle. Kayaking equipment, complete with flares, a fingerprinting demo from a real live detective, and a firefighter uniform brought in by the fire chief all added to the enjoyment of the tales. The kids asked a University of Rhode Island football player for his autograph when he came in to read, then asked a teacher for his autograph after he read coyote legends to them.

Perhaps the most interesting form of reading outside curriculum time came from a high school librarian in Wisconsin, who had attended a seminar in which I laid out the program and encouraged attendees to adapt it to their own situation. Months later, she sent me an e-mail detailing her approach. Free time was very limited in her school, so in order to make the greatest impact she asked herself who would most benefit from such a program. What identifiable group in many high schools most needs to be read to? Her answer was stunning: the football team.

This high school librarian asked the coach if she could ride the away-game bus with the varsity football team. When the bus left the parking lot for the first away game, without warning or introduction she stood up and began to read. The effect, she reported, was something akin to a fire drill. Heads popped up and concerned faces were turned toward her, but once the players understood what was happening they settled into one of two postures: they either draped themselves across the benches in front of them and listened with rapt attention, or they settled in and went to sleep. She read all the way out, then put a bookmark at her stopping point, and after the game she read all the way back home. She read coming and going to all the away games that season.

The coaches, she reported, were as happy with the results as the players. For most teams, the away record is worse than the home record. This is at least in part because the players spend the entire bus ride frittering away energy, throwing shoulder pads around and hitting each other over the head with their helmets. The players on this team arrived focused, relaxed, and at least in some cases quite well rested.

If that librarian had the courage and creativity to read to the high school varsity football team on the away bus, then every one of us can find a time to read to kids. There are lunches, indoor recesses during inclement weather, holidays, and summer breaks. Reading opportunities exist in schools, at camps, at the beach, and in the shopping mall. The need is there for teachers, parents, librarians, and just interested community members.

And this approach does not have to stop at reading. Jennifer Allen, a literacy specialist at the Albert S. Hall School in Waterville, Maine, used a similar approach in running a lunchtime writing program for fourth- and fifth-grade boys. The program was actually instituted by the boys, the majority of whom were struggling readers and reluctant classroom writers. Once a week for the whole school year, they got together and wrote. There were no assignments, no lessons, not even an expectation that the boys would finish anything, just a chance to share their writing and write together. Allen reported that she was largely invisible; the boys set their own social rules and drove the program. It is not what she would have envisioned for a writing program, but she was thrilled with the results.[5]

Schools are recognizing the opportunity of accomplishing double the good by having older children and teens read to younger children. There is great value in such an approach, although that value is diluted when schools reflexively recruit the best students—the National Honor Society member and the like—to be the readers. What the younger students really need is the role modeling of struggling students. Everybody wants to see someone who looks like them, so if the ultimate goal is to encourage struggling young readers, then it makes sense to pair them with struggling older readers. The experience holds promise for the struggling older readers as well. Many of them desperately need to be reading at their natural reading level, which is well below their grade level. Reading what could be seen as "kiddie" books carries a social stigma. But if the struggling reader is carrying a younger book and reading it for practice—and he is doing this because he is helping a needy younger student—then he is not being dumb, he is being a hero.

A friend of mine took a troop of Boy Scouts to their national jamboree, and knowing that such events are largely practice for how to stand in line, he brought a book. Whenever the troop was caught in line, he pulled out the book and started reading. Sometimes the boys forgot what they were waiting to do, or they simply chose to hear the rest of the story. Other troops began sidling over whenever he began reading. When will leaders at such events begin organizing armies of volunteers to station themselves at bottlenecks and make the most of these precious, and highly socializing, opportunities?

AUDIOBOOKS

We have another way for children to be read to as well, one our public libraries understand well. Libraries have long bemoaned the absence of male patrons between kindergarten age and retirement age. One of the ways we have brought this demographic back into the public library is by offering audiobooks. Certainly these are available to women as well, but the largest part of the audience for these collections is adult, working-age males. Imagine if you asked any of these men, mostly commuters, as they reached for a book on cassette or compact disk, if they would like to have someone read them a story. Their response would most likely be, no, I don't want you to read me a story, just give me my audiobook and let me go.

Being read to or listening to an audiobook—what is the difference? The difference is reading in isolation. Many men, used to using reading as their cave activity, their chance at separation, connect with an audiobook. They can get into their car, close the door, slip in a CD, and spend a solitary hour enjoying a low-pressure form of reading. If men react so well to this format, does it not make sense that boys would as well? Remember that hearing a story read out loud offers many of the positive results of reading itself. We can use audiobooks to greatly increase the amount of reading a boy hears. We should continue to read to boys as well, since the socialization and role modeling have value in themselves, but audiobooks promise volume as well as the opportunity to hear professional readers imbue books with passion and clarity.

THE STORYTELLER

The ultimate venue for exposing boys to story is oral storytelling. It is story in the purest of forms, without undue characterization and description and without the difficulties of the written word to stand between boys and the story they need.

Historically, storytelling served many of the roles that reading does today, back when reading materials were scarce and few people were literate. Storytelling served to transmit culture and social morays. It was used to educate, enrich, and entertain. Storytelling was news, history, and genealogy. Today, books, magazines, newspapers, and other mass media have taken the place of storytelling, and storytelling as an art is effectively dead. Harsh as that may sound, I as a professional storyteller spend most of my storytelling time acculturating audiences to the method of oral storytelling. Children seldom have any idea what is happening and so do not know how to react.

The modern world has abdicated storytelling to folk musicians and stand-up comedians. Who has the most to lose from the decline of traditional storytelling? Clearly it is those who still lack the skills to read effectively—and inordinately that means boys—who then turn to the media's passive, controlling forms that do little to train the mind to structured thinking. Storytelling is the better choice; it is more engaging and still rich enough in stimuli to appeal to the mind of a boy.

Companies today are beginning to recognize the power of oral storytelling to make their key personnel better communicators. If corporations are hiring professionals to make their executives storytellers, how can our schools, libraries, and community organizations be missing this trend? Storytelling is an idea whose time has come, again.

The power of storytelling came home to me on a day that, as the director of a public library, I was asked to give a speech to a local Rotary Club. Rotary can be a challenging audience. This was a midday speech to a group of mostly middle-age businessmen with incredibly busy schedules who had already sat through lunch and a business meeting and wanted nothing more than to get back to their offices and their sales calls. Add to that the fact that I was doing a children's story hour directly before the meeting, and that thanks to my busy schedule I had prepared nothing for my Rotary speech, and I was in for a long afternoon.

With no other ideas, I got up off the floor of the children's room after story hour, picked up a handful of the craft projects we had been doing, and left for the Rotary meeting. When I was introduced, I handed out the crafts to everyone in the room and proceeded to tell stories for twenty minutes, including some of the same stories I had told to the preschoolers. The effect was stunning. I have spoken before any number of service clubs; I never had an audience as rapt.

It all comes down to the Gatorade principle. After exercising for hours in the hot sun, you reach for that first bottle of Gatorade, tilt it to your lips, and what do you taste? Salt, that is what hits you. It could be seawater it is so salty, but it tastes wonderful because your body is seeking out what it really needs. An hour later, you reach for a second bottle and all you taste is sugar. Now it could be Kool-Aid. Those who lack the story they need in their life, whether they be elementary-age boys reading three years behind their classmates or fifty-year-old Rotarians, will react strongly to what they need.

Those who wish to become storytellers have many resources, including my earlier *Connecting Boys with Books* (American Library Association, 2003), which not only gives hints on learning storytelling but describes a detailed program to teach storytelling to students. Why teach storytelling? Schools have long emphasized differentiated instruction, meaning teaching in ways that speak to different learning styles and different intelligences. But this approach is becoming harder to implement as standardization and outside pressures limit teachers' flexibility in the classroom. And schools have never been able to fully implement differentiated assessment, which is allowing students to demonstrate their learning using different styles of communication. Even if a school succeeds in teaching to different learning styles, it can seldom do more to measure that learning than ask the children to fill in little bubbles on a standardized test.

Storytelling, in the hands of students, promises to be a vehicle for those with different learning styles to show their accomplishments. The traditional method of testing in schools seeks to learn what the student does not know. After all, teachers do not usually mark right answers on a test, only wrong ones. Storytelling allows students to show off what they do know. This is especially important for boys who often struggle with the written forms of language, which can mask their mastery of content. Researchers Kathy Sanford and Heather Blair identify types of literacy boys engage in, including "orally describing and explaining highly complex concepts." Further, they argue, "It is important that all students . . . be taught *and tested* in ways that . . . focus on their ability rather than their disability. . . . the dominant model of teaching and testing is to determine the student's weaknesses . . . and to remediate those weaknesses."[6]

When we consider boys and reading, we should remember that reading is a vehicle. Story is the cargo. But, like a tanker truck full of fuel, the cargo can be used to make the vehicle go. Expose boys to story and they will become better readers, and the better they are at reading, the more story they will encounter.

Books for Literary Lunch Beginners

Coville, Bruce. *Aliens Ate My Homework.* Aladdin, 2007.

Elliott, David. *The Transmogrification of Roscoe Wizzle.* Candlewick, 2004.

Korman, Gordon. *The Chicken Doesn't Skate.* Hyperion Books for Children, 1998.

Roberts, Ken. *The Thumb in the Box.* Groundwood Books, 2002.

Sachar, Louis. *Sideways Stories from Wayside School.* HarperTeen, 2004.

Spinelli, Jerry. *Loser.* HarperTrophy, 2003.

Sullivan, Michael. *Escapade Johnson and Mayhem at Mount Moosilauke.* Big Guy Books, 2006.

Van Draanen, Wendelin. *Swear to Howdy.* Yearling, 2005.

Books for Reading on the Football Team Bus

Deuker, Carl. *Gym Candy.* Houghton Mifflin, 2007.

Feinstein, John. *Cover-Up: Mystery at the Super Bowl.* Knopf, 2007.

Green, Tim. *Football Genius.* HarperCollins, 2007.

Lupica, Mike. *Two-Minute Drill.* Philomel, 2007.

Books on Reading Out Loud and Storytelling

MacDonald, Margaret Read. *The Storyteller's Start-Up Book: Finding, Learning, Performing and Using Folktales.* August House, 1993.

Sawyer, Ruth. *The Way of the Storyteller.* Viking Press, 1942; Penguin Reprint, 1977.

Shedlock, Marie L. *The Art of the Story-Teller.* D. Appleton, 1915; Kessinger, 2004.

Trelease, Jim. *The Read Out Loud Handbook.* 6th ed. Penguin, 2006.

Notes

1. Stephen Krashen, *The Power of Reading* (Westport, CT: Libraries Unlimited, 2004), 77–81.

2. Christina Clark and Kate Rumbold, *Reading for Pleasure: A Research Overview* (National Literacy Trust, 2006), 24.

3. *Guys Read Pilot Program: Final Report* (Fairbanks North Star Borough Public Library, 2007), 4.

4. Ibid., 5–7.

5. Jennifer Allen, "My Literary Lunches with Boys," *Educational Leadership,* September 2006, 67–70.

6. Kathy Sanford, Heather Blair, and Raymond Chodzinski, "A Conversation about Boys and Literacy," *Teaching and Learning,* Spring 2007, 7, 9 (emphasis added).

Chapter 6

Honoring Boys' Literature

The biggest obstacle to boys' reading is almost certainly the rift in perception between what boys consider reading and what the adults in their lives consider reading. Most of those who define "good" reading are female, and virtually everyone who does is an adult. Many educators and parents bemoan the fact that they just do not understand boys' reading; they just don't get it. We are not supposed to—we are not twelve-year-old boys. Still, we must try to understand, not just what boys read but how they read, and why.

Boys tend to connect with periodical literature, such as magazines and newspapers. These types of reading often involve short passages that have immediate application. They are more up to date than other types of reading, which seems to be of some importance to boys. Mostly, boys read periodical literature because that is what they see men read. A 1996 study asked kids which parent reads more books; respondents named their mothers ten times more than their fathers. When they were asked which parent reads more newspapers, their answers were reversed; the children pointed toward their fathers ten times more often than their mothers.[1]

A *Time* magazine study in 2005 showed men reading fewer magazines and more online content, including online magazines: "Men aren't migrating so much from the content of magazines as from the format."[2] Those who work with boys, and who understand that boys' reading often mirrors men's reading, would do well to keep track of this trend.

The types of reading boys value, such as digital reading, are often overlooked by teachers.[3] Boys often do not read books at all, and when they do it is often not the books we want them to read. Perhaps there is no clearer example of the wide gap between boys and educators in their outlook about reading, and the devastating effect this gap has on young readers' motivation, than a 2001 survey by the Young Adult Library Services Association. That survey asked teens how much they read, and for those who answered that they did not read, it followed by asking why. Far from the more clichéd answers—competition from the media and video games, busy schedules, and social pressure—the number one reason teens themselves gave for not reading was that reading is boring.[4] If there is any truth in their answers, then we should be able to change their minds about reading by giving them something interesting to read.

Many educators bemoan how little boys read, especially how little they read in books, but most can readily identify the kinds of books boys tend to enjoy reading. The fact that boys do not often connect what they read with what adults, especially educators, consider to be real reading suggests that we communicate to boys our disdain for their reading. It is worth while to explore the types of books that appeal to large numbers of boys, to understand both the reason for this appeal and our reluctance, for reasons real or imagined, to honor that reading.

On a cautionary note, we should always remind ourselves that these are generalities. Not all boys react to these types of literature, and these literatures appeal to some girls. It is vital that we take these generalities as instructive, not normative. The hope is that we can use them as tools for connecting kids with books. The fear should be that by identifying a type of literature with maleness we stigmatize boys who have other tastes and outlooks as being inappropriate and feminized. The goal is to make it clear that all tastes in reading are honored; excessive zeal can produce the opposite result if we are not vigilant.

SOME POINTS ON BOYS' READING

Remembering that girls tend to internalize and boys tend to externalize (see chapter 3), and that girls tend to see the world operating on interpersonal communication and cooperation while boys see the world operating on impersonal rules and realities, we should seriously consider what these differences in outlook mean for boys' reading.[5] Too often, when we think about reading for children, we focus on the juvenile novel. The basics of the novel are that a central character, a protagonist, must address an internal issue, usually with the help of other characters, and emerge at the end a changed, better person. This formula has appeal to educators who think reading should help children grow. The term we use is *bibliotherapy,* an approach that embodies what most educators want children to gain from their reading. Unfortunately, the juvenile novel is inherently inward-looking, focused on character interaction and self-reflection. It has little appeal to many boys, especially those who show the most typical boy outlook, the same boys who are most likely to have trouble reading.

The juvenile novel may be the basic form presented to children as high-quality reading, but if we as educators find that a boy does not respond well to this form there is a vast world of reading out there to choose from. Much of this literature gets little respect in educational circles, even though many of its forms have great appeal to many boys. The reason is simple: we as educators want children to read the best books, and so we present children with the books that speak to us, those books that have changed our lives. We forget sometimes that most of "we" arc women. It is not an issue of discrimination but one of perspective. We forget sometimes that there may be a different point of view out there, and so we fail to connect many boys with the books that may make them rabid readers. We need to realize that our distinctions about what makes a good book are likely based on narrow perspectives. We need to do more than free boys to choose their own reading matter; we need to communicate to them that their reading counts.

When we consider what boys read—and how they read, for that matter—there are some generalities to keep in mind. We should be careful not to use the terms *literature, fiction,* and *novel* as if they mean the same thing. Our literature for children includes both fiction and nonfiction, and fiction contains novels and the various genres. Boys tend to favor genre fiction, because it tends to be more plot-based than your basic novel, which tends to be more character-based.

Boys' readings are often short, because they tend to read below grade level and shorter books seem to be less of a chore. Many boys are drawn to series books, again to limit the struggles associated with reading. The hardest ten pages of any book are the first ten; that is when the reader must become accustomed to the writing style, setting, dialect, and a hundred other factors. With a series, the boy must go through that process only once and can then enjoy the rest of the series. Also, for boys who find little reading of interest, series give them the prospect of always having the next book when they do find something they like. Unfortunately, series tend to get little respect. One commentator in *Booklist* noted, "In the family of children's literature, fiction series books are often considered distant stepchildren, that is, if they are considered at all."[6]

Boys are often attracted to edgy reading, in whatever format they find it. We all see it but maybe do not try hard enough to understand why this is. Too often we dismiss this tendency as acting out. Boys see the world as operating on rules, on limits. They want to explore as wide a world as they can find, and how do they find out where the lines are if they do not dance over them every now and then? Thus, boys often explore the extremes in many aspects of their lives; literature is one area where we can support their explorations. Alison Follos describes it this way:

Edgy subject matter may feel like it's sending a confused or conflicting message, but the content is out there. The scariest fiction allows teens a vicarious experience, a forewarning from a safe zone, and anyone familiar with inner-city street life will attest that the real side of scary can be fatal. Having youth read "all about it" is preferable to living some of it.[7]

Bruce Coville "maintains that little 'appropriate' literature for young boys was written prior to his books. His observation is that young boys are by nature mischievous and they want to read about male characters who do 'naughty' not nasty things."[8] Is it hard to understand the appeal of the naughty? You are not supposed to understand it, because you are not the target audience. You are not a twelve-year-old boy.

NONFICTION

When we talk about the types of reading that have boy appeal, we first and foremost need to speak of nonfiction. Teachers, librarians, and parents often see a boy with a nonfiction book in hand and respond, "That's fine, now get a book you can read." Boys often see nonfiction not as a vehicle for finding specific information but as a way to better understand the world around them, to acquire the rules and tools they so desire. In short, they read nonfiction the way we expect children to read fiction. Adult men see nonfiction the same way. An all-men's reading club in Roanoke, Virginia, celebrated for its vibrancy and lasting power, chooses nonfiction for half of its books.[9]

Ray Doiron of the University of Prince Edward Island observed ten thousand free-reading choices made by children in grades one through six from their classroom libraries. Boys in his study chose three nonfiction books for every four fiction books. That finding, in and of itself, should tell us how important nonfiction is in the life of the boy reader. In addition, Doiron looked at the books in the classroom libraries involved and found that more than 85 percent of them were fiction.[10] Boys, when given free range, found almost half their reading in nonfiction, despite the fact that there was scant nonfiction to choose from. This study should also caution us; the fact that these classroom libraries were more than 85 percent fiction tells us how easy it is for us adults to underestimate the value of nonfiction.

Many nonfiction books give boys back an important part of their reading, one that they lost early in their school years—illustrations. Pictures can be a powerful stimulant to a boy's brain, and because of differences in brain structure boys benefit from stimuli in their environment when doing upper-level thinking, such as reading.[11] Illustrations also help children read at a higher level by giving visual clues to aid comprehension.[12] Boys rely more on these clues than girls do, partly because such clues stimulate the right side of the brain, which tends to be better developed in boys.[13]

VISUAL FICTION

If nonfiction is popular with boys partly because it gives them back their illustrations, it makes sense that boys would look to bring illustrations back into their fiction. There are various forms of visual fiction, such as Hudson Talbot's *Safari Journal: The Adventures in Africa of Carey Monroe* (Silver Whistle Books, 2003), which is laid out with words interspersed with photos, drawings, and comics. Big Guy Books, a small publisher from Carlsbad, California, has for some years produced the Time Soldiers series of chapter books, which mimics the picture book format but with photographs and computer-generated illustrations. Comic books have long been recognized as a popular boys' format.

Today, boys have the graphic novel format, book-length stories told in comic book fashion. Even more popular is manga, a Japanese-inspired format of serialized graphic fiction that looks like a bulky magazine. Too often parents, teachers, and librarians denigrate books with pictures automatically. The rise of graphic novels and manga is helping to reverse this trend, but these formats are often looked at as stepping-stones, as having value only if they lead to "real" reading later on. If this attitude is expressed to children, they too will come to believe, as they have with comic books, that these formats do not constitute "real reading."

HUMOR

Humor is a powerful tool for reaching boys. Many boys understand that they do not read up to grade level or as well as their classmates. They often face the concern, or consternation, of adults who worry about their lack of reading and pressure them to change their ways. The stress involved seldom helps. Humor is a great release for boys, turning a chore into a pleasure. For this reason, they often seek out edgy humor, responding to the constriction of adults by seeking release in the forbidden. The fact that adults often despise their choice of reading materials only adds to its appeal.

Adults may sometimes enjoy humor for kids, but it is always suspect and we tend to shy away from offering it to children unless it is squeaky clean, and you can spell that boring. Jon Scieszka, the great boys' humorist, is quoted as saying, "I can't think of a funny book that my kids ever had to read in school."[14] When Jeffrey Wilhelm and Michael Smith surveyed forty-nine boys about their connection to reading, none of their respondents could remember reading anything they thought was funny in school.[15]

Robert Fulghum, well known as a writer of wise and wry humor for adults, wrote in the last chapter of his book *It Was on Fire When I Lay Down on It* that after writing that book he actually considered going back and taking out all the funny parts. He noted, "Humor is a bit suspect—conventional wisdom says it takes away from serious writing."[16] If even the author of *All I Really Need to Know I Learned in Kindergarten* (Villard, 1988) must be uncomfortable about humor, how do we expect boys to respect it?

FANTASY AND SCIENCE FICTION

A friend of mine once called me over to discuss the reading habits of his son, whom he thought was in serious trouble. The father led me to his son's room and showed me a bookcase filled with paperback series fantasy. My friend explained that his boy would read through the entire bookcase every couple of months, then go back and read it all again. He told me that we needed to get his son away from fantasy or he would never become a reader. Looking at the bookcase that the teenager read through three or four times a year, I realized that the son in all likelihood read more than his father and I combined.

Adults often see fantasy as a stepping-stone, acceptable only if it leads to more serious, "real" reading. Science fiction tends to get even less respect. One researcher's son told her that some of his teachers treated sci-fi books like they were pornography.[17] Why this indifference, and even hostility, to these forms? Educators tend to value the inward journey more than the outward, physical journey. We want children looking inward, to learn self-reflection and self-examination. Although these are noble goals, embodied in the form of the juvenile novel, they are also in line with a typical female point of view. Girls tend to internalize, looking inward for their understanding of the world. Boys tend to look outward, placing themselves in a larger world.

Many adults dismiss fantasy as escapist, often forgetting how much many adults value escapist literature. Girls, it is commonly noted, are more drawn to realistic fiction. The case of fantasy is more complex, though. Boys often find fantasy dealing with real issues in their lives, issues they find difficult to talk about, giving them the freedom to explore such issues with an emotional distance, or comfort zone.[18]

In a study of boys choosing books on their own at a large bookstore, a researcher noted that "for all of the boys, the escapist qualities of imaginative fiction were strongly preferred over the immediate connections to their lives that young adult realistic fiction might provide."[19] Science fiction and fantasy have great appeal to many boys because their basic structure is so much in opposition to the standard juvenile novel. These forms begin with the concept of an individual discovering a new world and journeying out to find a place in that world.

SPORTS, ACTION, AND ADVENTURE

Boys are active creatures, and they seek to connect their reading to what they like. They want to read about characters doing what they enjoy, and think they would enjoy, doing. Sports and action/adventure stories are plot driven, not character driven. The action in the story takes precedence over characterization, character interaction, and character development. Many adults dismiss these stories because they are so external, so physical, and not inward or reflective.

GOTHIC HORROR

In this post-Columbine era, our society is very sensitive to the presence, or even the discussion of, violence around children. We believe that any exposure to violence increases the likelihood that children will engage in violence, especially if those children are male. What, then, are we to make of the fascination so many boys have with gothic horror and its graphic portrayals of violence? We need to step back and realize that violence is a fact in the world, and boys being external thinkers seek to understand the world around them. Violence, indeed, can be such an anomalous factor that boys need to address it in order to find their balance.

Boys see violence in the media, in their communities, even in their homes. School librarian Alison Follos reports that in a single year an avid thirteen-year-old television watcher witnesses seven thousand screen murders.[20] Violence is unavoidable, but it cannot remain unexplained. Boys can either face the fact of violence in the more visual media, to which language is ill suited, or they can do it in books, where narration can give context and highlight consequences.

Encountering violence in a narrative context may help boys learn to cope with violence rather than encourage them to engage in it. Sometimes we have to just get over it.

CODED LANGUAGE

Boys are often attracted to coded language—to riddles, puzzles, word games, and the like. Such reading is short and challenging to the mind, and often requires more thinking than actual reading. In addition, it turns language into a game. It also levels the playing field for boys who struggle with language. Boys may not understand coded language right off the bat, but neither does anyone else. For once, they are on an even footing.

NO MORE DEAD DOGS

What do all the aforementioned forms that appeal to boys have in common? Adults, especially educators, give them little respect. The disdain for the outward and physical over the inward and emotional, the fear of edginess and violence, and the denigration of humor all help to explain why so many educators look down at boys' favored reading material. Sports books, action/adventure, and gothic horror gain little respect from adults. How do we know this? How often do these traditionally boy-friendly formats find their way onto book award or school reading assignment lists?

Gordon Korman, a children's author who consistently produces books with high boy appeal, is fond of asking audiences to consider how many books there are on the Newbery Award list with an extremely slim plot element, namely, the death of a beloved dog, compared to truly funny books. Korman based an entire book on this concept, *No More Dead Dogs* (Hyperion, 2000). Most educators can name a handful of books considered to be among the best books for kids with this incredibly thin plot element. Consider *Sounder,* by William H. Armstrong, a Newbery Medal winner in 1970; *Old Yeller,* by Fred Gipson, a Newbery Honor Book in 1957; *Where the Red Fern Grows,* by Wilson Rawls, which should count twice since two dogs meet their mortal end in that book; and more recently Sherman Alexie's *The Absolutely True Diary of a Part-Time Indian,* which won a National Book Award in 2008.

Conversely, there may be Newbery Award winners with humor, but there are none that are predominantly funny books. The same test can be applied to all boy-friendly forms. How many sports books carry the coveted gold seal?

How many action/adventure stories? A quick check of the subject headings attached to the Newbery Medal winners in the twenty years from 1989 to 2008 shows no nonfiction at all. The last nonfiction title to win was *Lincoln: A Photobiography,* by Russell Freedman, in 1988. Before that you have to go back to *Daniel Boone,* by James Daugherty, which won in 1940. In the past twenty years, no fantasy book has won the award, no book of gothic horror, and no action/adventure title. One science fiction title has won, but then again so have one fairy tale, one book of drama, and two books of poetry.

There are four books of medieval fiction among the last twenty Newbery Medal winners, three books on death, two about runaways, two about orphans, and three about depressions (the economic kind). Depression of the psychological kind seems almost universal: library catalogs identify books about grandmothers, aunts, sisters, homelessness, abandoned children, disabilities, childbirth, and grief among these twenty books. Although there are no very recent dead dog books on the list, there are dogs that are pitifully ugly, abused, and bitten by a rattlesnake. In the National Book Award winner, Alexie's *The Absolutely True Diary of a Part-Time Indian,* the dog is shot by the physically challenged and mentally injured ethnic boy's alcoholic father. Clearly, if you want good reviews, it makes more sense to include a plethora of issues than too many laughs.

Is there anything wrong with these heavily used themes? Not at all, but the pattern is both clear and troublesome. There is a definite bias toward the types of books that traditionally appeal to girls. This bias appears in other awards lists as well. During a survey of teen boys' choices in a bookstore, the researcher compared the ninety books chosen by the boys in the study to the ninety books listed on the International Reading Association's Young Adults' Choices project book lists from the preceding three years. There was absolutely no overlap of titles. Indeed, there were only two authors who showed up in both lists. For this researcher, "The relatively minuscule representation of young adult realistic fiction among the boys' preferred texts only highlights the contrast."[21] The best-books list he had studied, as is the case with so many, is dominated by character-driven juvenile novels. This bias is just as apparent on many summer reading lists and in just about every case where we present the best books for children. The constant, cumulative reinforcement of this idea, that the types of books that appeal to boys are not good books, cannot help but affect the way boys see reading.

James Howe summarizes this idea in his satire for children, *Screaming Mummies of the Pharaoh's Tomb II.* Two of his characters, both happening to be dogs, are collaborating on a book, but they disagree about what kind of book to write.

Delilah, the female dog, tries to explain to Howie, the male dog, what would give the book the best chance of winning a Newbony Award. "Books that are sad and take place a long time ago. It also helps if the characters are poor and somebody dies, or if the main character, usually a child and preferably an orphan, goes on a long journey. Alone. Oh, and it should be a book girls will like."[22]

We fail to honor boys' reading, not because we do not care about boys, but because their reading material does not speak to us. One school librarian, female, put it this way: "As a person, like many of you, who enjoys reading nearly everything, it's easy to pathologize boys who have reading preferences so different than mine."[23] What it comes down to is that, too often, we care too much. We know that boys do not read as much or as well as girls; we know we might have only one chance to influence them. Hence, we hesitate to promote books that we do not respect. If that boy reads only one book this year, our reasoning goes, it is not going to be *Captain Underpants*! What we fail to realize sometimes is that, if he reads *Captain Underpants,* he just might read two books this year, and for many boys that will be a victory. To those who worry that boys' reading is too narrow, too restricted by gender stereotypes, researcher William Brozo argues that "concern for listless and struggling male readers must take precedence for teacher and parents alike."[24]

The point is not that boys should be allowed to read anything, no matter how worthless it is, just so long as they are reading. If that is what you believe, you will almost certainly transmit that attitude in some way to the boys you are trying to help, further convincing them that they are bad readers. They are not. A survey specifically targeting successful teen boy readers confirmed the same tendencies to choose this "boys' literature" among this advanced subsection on all points except periodicals and humor.[25] The point is not that boys read bad books, it is that the books boys find value in thereby have value. The fact that you do not see the value is irrelevant; you are not the target audience. Boys' literature does exist, and it is a world we have to go out into and come to grips with if we are going to help boys become lifelong readers.

Nonfiction Books for Boys

Chin, Karen, and Thom Holmes. *Dino Dung: The Scoop on Fossil Feces.* Random House, 2005.

Fleischman, John. *Phineas Gage: A Gruesome but True Story about Brain Science.* Houghton Mifflin, 2002.

Fleisher, Paul. *Parasites: Latching On to a Free Lunch.* Twenty-First Century Books, 2006.

Gurstelle, William. *Backyard Ballistics.* Chicago Review Press, 2001.

Holtz, Thomas R., and Luis V. Rey. *Dinosaurs: The Most Complete, Up-to-Date Encyclopedia for Dinosaur Lovers of All Ages.* Random House, 2007.

Lewis, Michael. *The Blind Side: Evolution of a Game.* Norton, 2007.

Markle, Sandra. *Outside and Inside Mummies.* Walker Books for Young Readers, 2005.

Masoff, Joy. *Oh Yuck! The Encyclopedia of Everything Nasty.* Workman Publishing, 2000.

Piven, Joshua, and David Borgenicht. *The Worst-Case Scenario Survival Handbook: Extreme Edition.* Chronicle Books, 2005.

Silverstein, Ken. *The Radioactive Boy Scout: The True Story of a Boy and His Backyard Nuclear Reactor.* Villard, 2005.

Singer, Marilyn. *What Stinks?* Darby Creek Publishing, 2006.

Solheim, James. *It's Disgusting and We Ate It! True Food Facts from around the World and throughout History.* Simon and Schuster Children's Publishing, 1998.

Solway, Andrew. *What's Living in Your Bedroom?* Heinemann Library, 2004.

Woodford, Chris, and Jon Woodcock. *Cool Stuff 2.0 and How It Works.* Dorling Kindersley, 2007.

Humor Books for Boys

Blacker, Terence. *Boy 2 Girl.* Farrar, Straus and Giroux, 2005.

Colfer, Eoin. *The Legend of Spud Murphy.* Miramax, 2004.

Gantos, Jack. Joey Pigza series. HarperTrophy.

Garfinkle, D. L. Supernatural Rubber Chicken series. Mirrorstone.

Gleitzman, Morris. *Toad Rage.* Yearling, 2005.

Hiaasen, Carl. *Hoot.* Yearling, 2006.

Korman, Gordon. *Schooled.* Hyperion, 2007.

Moore, Christopher. *Lamb: The Gospel According to Biff, Christ's Childhood Pal.* Harper Paperbacks, 2003.

Nelson, Blake. *Gender Blender.* Delacorte Books for Young Readers, 2007.

Smallcomb, Pam. *The Last Burp of Mac McGerp.* Bloomsbury, 2004.

Strasser, Todd. *Is That a Dead Dog in Your Locker?* Scholastic, 2008.

Sullivan, Michael. Escapade Johnson series. PublishingWorks.

Sports Books for Boys

Feinstein, John. *Last Shot: A Final Four Mystery.* Knopf, 2005.

Grisham, John. *Playing for Pizza.* Doubleday, 2007.

Gutman, Dan. Baseball Card Adventures series. HarperCollins.

Lupica, Mike. *The Big Field*. Penguin, 2008.

Martino, Alfred C. *Pinned*. Harcourt, 2005.

Paulsen, Gary. *How Angel Peterson Got His Name, and Other Outrageous Tales of Extreme Sports*. Yearling, 2004.

Ritter, John H. *The Boy Who Saved Baseball*. Philomel, 2003.

Skuy, David. *Off the Crossbar*. Writer's Collective, 2006.

Science Fiction Books for Boys

Anderson, M. T. *Feed*. Candlewick, 2004.

DuPrau, Jeanne. *The City of Ember*. Yearling, 2004.

Oppel, Kenneth. Matt Cruse series. Eos.

Patterson, James. Maximum Ride series. Little, Brown and Company.

Philbrick, Rodman. *The Last Book in the Universe*. Blue Sky Press, 2002.

Schusterman, Neal. *Unwind*. Simon and Schuster, 2007.

Stead, Rebecca. *First Light*. Wendy Lamb Books, 2007.

Weaver, Will. *Defect*. Farrar, Straus and Giroux, 2007.

Fantasy Books for Boys

Delaney, Michael. The Last Apprentice series. Greenwillow.

Duey, Kathleen. A Resurrection of Magic series. Atheneum.

Farmer, Nancy. *The House of the Scorpion*. Atheneum, 2002.

Flanagan, John. The Ranger's Apprentice series. Philomel.

Hearn, Lian. Tales of the Otori series. Puffin.

Humphries, Chris. The Runestone Saga series. Knopf.

Pratchett, Terry. *Thud*. HarperTorch, 2006.

Riordan, Rick. Percy Jackson and the Olympians series. Hyperion.

Stone, Jeff. The Five Ancestors series. Random House.

Stroud, Jonathan. The Bartimaeus Trilogy series. Miramax.

Ward, David. The Grassland Trilogy series. Amulet Books.

Gothic Horror Books for Boys

Jenkins, A. M. *Night Road*. HarperTeen, 2008.

Horowitz, Anthony. The Gatekeepers series. Scholastic.

Kehlert, Peg. *The Ghost's Grave*. Puffin, 2007.

Moore, Christopher. *Dirty Job*. William Morrow, 2006.

Shan, Darren. The Demonata series. Little, Brown Young Readers.

Spignesi, Stephen. *The Weird 100: A Collection of the Strange and the Unexplained.* Citadel Press, 2004.

Teitelbaum, Michael. *The Scary States of America.* Delacorte Books for Young Readers, 2007.

Action/Adventure Books for Boys

Bruchac, Joseph. *Code Talker: A Novel about the Navajo Marines of World War Two.* Speak, 2005.

Gutman, Dan. *Getting Air.* Simon and Schuster, 2007.

Hobbs, Will. *Go Big or Go Home.* HarperCollins, 2008.

Horowitz, Anthony. Alex Rider Adventures series. Philomel.

Korman, Gordon. Everest series. Scholastic.

Mikaelsen, Ben. *Touching Spirit Bear.* HarperTeen, 2005.

Philbrick, Rodman. *The Young Man and the Sea.* Scholastic Paperbacks, 2005.

Salisbury, Graham. *Night of the Howling Dogs.* Wendy Lamb Books, 2007.

Strasser, Todd. Drift X series. Simon Pulse.

Notes

1. Donald D. Pottorff, Deborah Phelps-Zientarski, and Michelle E. Skovera, "Gender Perceptions of Elementary and Middle School Students about Literacy at Home and School," *Journal of Research and Development in Education,* Summer 1996, 211.

2. Jon Fine, "Where the Boys Aren't." *BusinessWeek,* November 7, 2005, 24.

3. Kathy Sanford, Heather Blair, and Raymond Chodzinski, "A Conversation about Boys and Literacy," *Teaching and Learning,* Spring 2007, 5.

4. Patrick Jones and Dawn Cartwright Fiorelli, "Overcoming the Obstacle Course: Teenage Boys and Reading," *Teacher Librarian,* February 2003, 10.

5. Eva M. Pomerantz, Ellen Rydell Altermatt, and Jill L. Saxon, "Making the Grade but Feeling Distressed: Gender Differences in Academic Performance and Internal Distress," *Journal of Educational Psychology,* June 2002, 396.

6. Michael O. Tunnell and James S. Jacobs, "Series Fiction and Young Readers," *Booklist,* September 15, 2005, 64.

7. Alison M. G. Follos, *Reviving Reading: School Library Programming, Author Visits and Books That Rock!* (Westport, CT: Libraries Unlimited, 2006), 10.

8. Judith A. Morley and Sandra E. Russell, "Making Literature Meaningful: A Classroom/Library Partnership," in *Battling Dragons: Issues and Controversy in Children's Literature,* by Susan Lehr (Portsmouth, NH: Heinemann, 1995), 260.

9. Karen Dillon, "No Girls Allowed: Men Bond over Books," *Roanoke Times,* August 3, 2007, C1.

10. Roy Doiron, "Boy Books, Girl Books," *Teacher Librarian,* February 2003, 14.

11. Carla Hannaford, *Smart Moves: Why Learning Is Not All in Your Head* (Arlington, VA: Great Ocean Publishers, 1995), 80.

12. Jeffrey D. Wilhelm and Michael Smith, "Asking the Right Questions: Literate Lives of Boys," *Reading Teacher,* May 2005, 788.

13. Michael Gurian, *Boys and Girls Learn Differently! A Guide for Teachers and Parents* (San Francisco: Jossey-Bass, 2002), 49.

14. Greg Toppo, "Funny, but Boys Do Read," *USA Today,* July 6, 2005, Life, 8d.

15. Wilhelm and Smith, "Asking the Right Questions," 788.

16. Robert Fulghum, *It Was on Fire When I Lay Down on It* (New York: Villard, 1989), 217.

17. Donna Lester Taylor, "'Not Just Boring Stories': Reconsidering the Gender Gap for Boys," *Journal of Adolescent and Adult Literacy,* December/January 2005, 293.

18. Wilhelm and Smith, "Asking the Right Questions," 788.

19. Sean Cavazos-Kottke, "Five Readers Browsing: The Reading Interests of Talented Middle School Boys," *Gifted Child Quarterly,* Spring 2006, 144.

20. Follos, *Reviving Reading,* 11.

21. Cavazos-Kottke, "Five Readers Browsing," 144.

22. James Howe, *Screaming Mummies of the Pharaoh's Tomb II* (New York: Atheneum Books for Young Readers, 2003), 6.

23. Sandra Lingo, "The All Guys Book Club: Where Boys Take the Risk to Read," *Library Media Connection,* April/May 2007, 25.

24. William G. Brozo, *To Be a Boy, to Be a Reader* (Newark, DE: International Reading Association, 2002.), 19.

25. Cavazos-Kottke, "Five Readers Browsing," 144.

Chapter 7

Promoting Reading to Boys

A colleague of mine, a public librarian, was called in for a conference by her sixth-grade son's teacher. Little Jeremy (not his real name) was your typical eleven-year-old boy—active, somewhat mischievous, and not known as one of the great English scholars of his generation. This year, though, he had started so well in English that his teacher was astounded. He aced every test, completed every homework assignment, and leapt energetically into class discussions. Then, a few weeks into the school year, everything changed. Suddenly he was back to his old ways, not doing homework, zoning out in class, failing every test miserably. It was time to have a sit-down with mom.

The teacher laid out the problem as she saw it, that Jeremy had simply lost focus, gotten lazy. He could do the work; that much was clear from his early performance. The mother pointed out that Jeremy had loved the first book the class read, *Maniac Magee,* by Jerry Spinelli (Little, Brown, 1999). Jeremy had actually done his homework twice most nights, reading the assigned passage, then going back to find the funny parts. He would follow his mother around the kitchen, reading aloud to her while she prepared dinner.

But when that book was done, Jeremy could not stomach the second book, *Julie of the Wolves,* by Jean Craighead George (HarperTeen, 2003). Not only did he not enjoy the book, but it addressed things about girls that he, a sixth-grade boy, simply did not want to know. He went so far as to try negotiating for extra chores if he would be allowed to skip his reading. The mother said to the teacher, "You have to understand, he really hates this book."

The teacher replied, "I know, the boys always do."

This sixth-grade teacher dismissed not only half of her class with a phrase, but half of every class for every year she assigned this book. The question must be asked, if she knows half her class will despise a book, why does she keep assigning it? The answer lies in how we think about kids and reading, and especially how we look at the books that appeal to boys as opposed to those that appeal to girls.

Ironically, if Jeremy had simply not responded to a book that did appeal to him, he may never have come to his teacher's attention and so could have avoided having his mother called in for a teacher conference. So often, we simply think of boys as nonreaders until we are proved wrong. If we look at results, we have good reason to do so.

The teacher had three reasons for assigning the book: First, she argued, the class had read a boy book and now they were being assigned a girl book. The boys had their chance; now they had to suck it up and give the girls a chance. Second, she thought it her duty to expose her students to reading that they would not do on their own. Last, she had to assign something for the class to read, didn't she?

I would (and will) argue with all three assertions.

A DIFFERENT WAY OF LOOKING AT IT

Maniac Magee is not a "boy book" just because boys like it; it is a book with broad appeal to both boys and girls. How different would the situation be if the teacher thought of it as a "girl book" because girls like it? Would she then have had to assign a great Ben Mikaelsen adventure story for her second book? It has been observed that girls are more likely to read a boy book, particularly one with a boy main character, than boys are to read a girl book. Therefore, a book that everybody likes can be called a boy book, but a book that only girls like is called a girl book. To adults, it may seem that boys are being unreasonably picky. From a boy's point of view, it seems that a boy book is defined by the fact that boys like it, even if girls like it as well, but a girl book is defined by the fact that boys hate it.

Many of the books adults consider to be boy friendly are ones that have some appeal to boys and some appeal to adults, a sort of middle-of-the-road approach. Although these books may have more appeal than the identifiable girl books, they are unlikely to have the kind of appeal that will tempt a boy for whom reading is considered a chore. It is often said that the definition of insanity is doing the same thing over and over again and expecting different results. For those boys who feel disconnected to reading, we need to be willing to offer books that really speak to boys, even if those books make us uncomfortable or leave us wondering what boys see in such literature.

The teacher's diversity argument seems more solid. We certainly would like to expose students to many different types of reading. The problem comes in the compulsion. If we are teaching students to take an honest approach toward this diverse reading, then it makes sense to offer it in a less didactic manner, or at least to allow students some level of choice about the diverse reading they attempt. If the goal is to improve reading itself, then breadth is not of great consequence. William Brozo, an expert in the field of curriculum reading, suggests that teachers would do well to help struggling students identify with texts that are already familiar to them.[1] It only makes sense. Boys will have already gravitated toward texts that have some meaning for them.

Researcher Sean Cavazos-Kottke points this out:

> A consistent theme in the literature on reading instruction for the gifted and talented is the importance of personal interest as a significant attitude towards reading. . . . Most scholarship on building reading programs for the gifted recommends that gifted readers be given some freedom . . . by self-selecting personally interesting materials.[2]

He goes on to suggest that, if this is good for the gifted, it should be offered to all.

The other part of the teacher's argument makes less sense. Do we indeed need to assign one book to an entire class? Absolutely not. Having a group of students read the same book, almost always fiction and usually a standard novel, and then sit around and talk about that book is a time-honored approach to teaching literature. It also mirrors the book clubs that seem to have so little appeal to men. If Dad would not engage in such an activity voluntarily, why do we assume that Junior will connect with such an approach?

CHILD-DRIVEN READING

Schools need to consider having at least some of their English or language arts time given over to free-reading assignments. The concept is simple: instead of giving the entire class the same book to read, assign everybody in the class to choose their own book. Have them check the book in with the teacher to assure that every child has a book, and then when the class would usually be discussing a group book have the children individually stand before the class and explain what they read and why they liked it. Cavazos-Kottke developed a program in this vein that came to be known as self-selected reading (as distinct from SSR, silent sustained reading). At first he tried various rules to govern selection, but finally he decided that the best rule was no rule at all and opened the doors to all forms and formats of reading. Amazingly, the program was instituted in an honors English class, not to help remedial readers. It seems that even among these skilled readers, especially the boys, there was a feeling of disconnectedness that needed to be addressed.[3]

Free-reading assignments like this are revolutionary in that they turn the direction of reading on its head. In our schools today, reading is largely adult directed, whether that direction comes from the teacher, the curriculum committee, the school board, or even state or national governing bodies. Free-reading assignments put some of that direction back into the hands of students, and self-directed readers are better readers. Brozo found that "choice and control are two ingredients commonly missing in instruction provided to adolescent boys who are not reading as would be expected for their grade level and who are disinterested and reluctant readers."[4] Shirley Brown and Paula Roy report a similar finding, that "boys who were labeled as struggling readers reported that they became interested in school-based literacy when they had teachers who were attentive and supportive and when they were given choice in their assignments."[5]

Free-reading assignments can do more, though, than simply validate boys' reading choices. Having kids recommend reading to one another is powerful. For many kids—especially boys—who have been behind in reading and view reading as an activity not for them, any book suggestion from an adult is suspect. Adults have been giving them books that are too hard and of little interest for their entire school career. They are much more likely to take a suggestion from a peer. Free reading, when done as a whole-class experience, turns every child into a reading advocate to his or her classmates.

Free-reading assignments also help dilute what many boys see as unfair assignment practices. Beyond the obvious bent of curriculum reading toward novels and away from nonfiction and the more plot-driven genres, many language arts teachers make a special assignment during the month of March to read a book written by a woman. The reason is simple enough: it is Women's History Month, and it makes sense to celebrate that through literature. What boys see, though, is an assignment to read a book by a woman when there is no assignment to read a book by a man. We adults may know that male authors are well represented in the canon of Western literature, but that is not the impression the boys have. We see it as diversity; they see it as discrimination. This is but one example; boys may find many inequalities, real or imagined, in the way we assign literature. Free-reading assignments help boys see reading as something more attuned to their needs.

LOOSENING UP

It is important not only to understand what boys read but to make boys understand that we honor their reading. But that still is not enough. We must promote reading in ways that speak to boys. Many educators and parents can understand the reasons behind boys' literature, but the fact that this literature means nothing to them makes it hard to go beyond simply putting the books on a bookshelf and walking away. How easy would it be for libraries in this country, public as well as school libraries, to simply single out a shelf and mark it "Books for Guys"? Are we that uptight about being gender neutral? One school to whom I suggested this idea found that the exercise of choosing the books itself was a powerful and productive program. It allowed the boys from the remedial reading program to gather and create the cart. The boys themselves named the process the "Book Frenzy."

In our classrooms, too, we need to recognize that boys read differently than girls. Girls, being more internal, read for reading's sake, whereas boys want to read for a purpose. This is one of the reasons boys so often fail to connect with schoolwork. Kathy Sanford and Heather Blair summarize what boys want to see in their school activities as "(a) personal interest, (b) action, (c) success, (d) fun, and (e) purpose. . . . Boys 'morph' school-based assignments so that these qualities exist for them."[6]

Sanford and Blair coined the phrase "morphing literacy" and defined it as

> how boys (in particular) make sense of and manipulate school-based
> tasks set for them so that the activities become meaningful and for some
> boys, bearable. . . . [They] use a humorous approach (bordering on the
> inappropriate), depicting rough play, violence, defiance of rules, and 'making
> fun' of situations . . . creation of fantasy situations and worlds, enabling
> characters to have superhuman powers or to act in ridiculous ways. . . . they
> are often not able to or interested in completing tasks for the teacher's praise;
> rather, their gratification comes from having fun, entertaining their peers,
> making tasks suit their own interests.[7]

If that is what boys do to make literacy meaningful to themselves in school, why do *we* not do the same to make literacy meaningful to them?

We need to recognize the role of gender in reading promotion if we hope to reach the boys who see reading as solitary, sedentary, and feminized. Can you think of three things less appealing to a ten-year-old boy? We need to take each of these preconceptions and make a concerted effort to discredit it.

ROLE MODELING

First, let us address the idea that reading is a solitary activity. The need for role modeling in reading is such that it must be addressed throughout our society. Everybody wants to see examples of someone who looks like them, and boys need support as they meet the challenge of reading. Remember, reading is one of the most difficult skills that we master in our lives, and we are expected to do it by the time we are eight years old. For boys, that is a double challenge, because they are expected to do it at a time when their brains are less developed than girls' brains. To connect boys to reading, we need men to show the way. Given that so many men are solitary readers, this will take a concerted effort in every area of our society.

I often challenge men who do not feel comfortable reading to boys to sit up in a chair on their front porches for half an hour a day, put a book over their faces, and fall asleep. Just the vision of a man with a book will do at least something to plant in boys' minds the idea of men and books together. I often challenge schools to institute a new dress code: every male working in the building must carry a paperback book in his back pocket at all times. I further instruct the female teachers to enforce this new rule by carrying paperback books and putting them in the pockets of men who fail to live up to their duty. We should not underestimate the importance of a little role modeling when it comes to boys' reading.

Certainly, symbolic role modeling is not as effective as actual male involvement in the reading lives of boys. It starts in the home, where too often the job of guiding young readers falls to the mothers. Men need to recognize their own importance to young boys, who can easily get the impression that only women read and only women teach reading. Not only can men read to their sons, they can help show boys that reading is part of a continuum of learning, that reading is a means toward any end they desire. This is reading from the male perspective. Men need to be guides to learning and teach boys that reading is the map.

Consequently, schools and libraries must make an effort to bring men in, and to connect reading with activities that men and boys like. Groups that do activities with boys need to make reading a part of their regular routine. Too often, reading is taught as an isolated, and isolating, activity. When outside activities are brought into schools and libraries, they are often of a sort not appealing to your average male, either child or adult. I will never forget the librarian who, on hearing my plea for enriching experiences in libraries, complained that she tried to bring men into her library but could never get any to come to her knitting programs.

ACTIVE LEARNING

We have to fight the idea that reading is inherently sedentary. Although we may cherish the idea of a child curled up in a corner with a book on a long, rainy afternoon, that is not the reality for many boys. Their ideas about reading, if indeed they have any, are more likely to center around reading for a brief period the instructions to a toy—a radio-controlled car or a video game perhaps—and then immediately putting that new knowledge to work. Later they may return to their reading for another short burst to be followed by even more activity.

When we discovered that girls were having problems in school, sinking to the back of an overly loud and competitive learning environment, we did not solve the problem by pumping all the girls full of steroids to make them more aggressive. We did not use behavior-altering drugs to make half of our students fit the classroom environment. Instead, we rearranged our classrooms to make them more accessible, and to give girls a better chance to succeed. Now that we see boys struggling in an environment that is ill suited to their learning style, do we rearrange our classrooms to help boys? Sadly, we do not. Instead, we pump them full of drugs to make them conform.[8] Remember, up to 95 percent of students coded as ADHD are male.

Many schools are experimenting with the concept of SSR, or silent sustained reading. The idea is to highlight the importance of reading by regularly setting aside large chunks of time to allow children to read undisturbed. Although the goal is admirable, the execution is often problematic. It highlights the way girls tend to read. If sitting still and concentrating for long periods of instruction are often hard for boys, then doing so for reading, without even the audio stimulus of the teacher's voice, is likely to be even harder. One teacher addressed this problem by simply allowing a boy to do his SSR while walking circles around the classroom.[9] That might be a little distracting to the other students, but the approach is note-worthy. Teaching special needs students, I often opened a large outdoor area for students to read in, knowing some at least would choose to read while walking.

Many boys benefit from simply being able to spread out while reading, on the floor or couches. Sometimes it is the silent part of silent sustained reading that is a problem; allow boys to listen to music, around a group radio or through headphones, while they read. Many educators may find that a bizarre thought—after all, how can one concentrate on a book with music running through his head? Still, many adult men read the newspaper in front of the television news or read a book while watching a baseball game. Sometimes that little bit of stimulus makes all the difference to the male brain.

Librarians and parents would do well to note these same approaches. Adolescent boys are often noticeable in their absence from libraries. Part of the reason is the library atmosphere, real or imagined, of quiet and restraint. Especially in the after-school hours—after boys have been cooped up, ordered about, and generally forced to repress any physical tendencies—the prospect of being shushed and herded into hard-backed chairs for a few hours at the public library may seem distasteful. Public and school libraries should work hard to differentiate some space, or at least some time, for a little noise and confusion. If nothing else, this accommodation helps differentiate the library from the classroom, where so many boys face discomfort and failure.

Battles often arise between parents and adolescent boys over proper study habits, and often what is at issue is the number of extra stimuli in the environment. Boys, knowing instinctively that they need to rouse their brains, seek stimuli and end up overcompensating. Parents, believing that the proper learning environment is quiet and orderly to the point of sterility, come down hard on any possible distractions.

Schools, libraries, and families alike need to recognize this different approach to reading and accept that it is neither better nor worse than the sustained reading often associated with girls. It is just a different form of literacy. The more we honor this different literacy, the more doors we open to many boys who have given up on reading.

BOOK GROUPS

Book discussion groups may appeal more to girls and women than to boys and men, but that has more to do with how we run them than any inherent properties of groups. Book groups can still be a great way to share and support reading. As in any reading promotion program, one option is to organize the program by gender. An all-boys reading group may allow a school, library, or community group to present a program that takes advantage of gender-specific tendencies, as indeed a corresponding all-girls program would. A program meant to be truly open to both genders should seek to honor different tendencies, acknowledging that the most traditional format for book discussions is heavily tilted toward a traditionally female point of view.

If we do everything we can to make book discussions as little like what we think book discussions should be, then we will be well on the road to making them more boy friendly. The Scott County Public Library in Georgetown, Kentucky, began a boys-only book club and named it the "Pig Skull Book Club," with an appropriately stark-looking visual. You had to join the group to get the explanation of the name. The club met on Sunday afternoons, a time more likely to fit the schedule of some working fathers who would be effectively barred from more common weekday afternoon programs. Just these few changes already set this program apart from your run-of-the-mill book discussion group. And that difference works; a year after its inception, the Pig Skull Book Club was alive and well, and the library had started satellite programs in some of the local schools.

We should begin with the physical layout of a book group. Too often, we set up chairs around a table, or just in a circle, and set kids to talking about a book. We need to understand a simple concept, that girls tend to speak face to face, and boys tend to speak best shoulder to shoulder. Consider a group of men hanging out at a Little League field. Most likely you see them either sitting on the bleachers, elbows resting on their knees, chins resting in their hands, or lined up and leaning against a fence. In either case, they are staring out into left field and apparently speaking to nobody. They are, of course, speaking to the men beside them. Speaking face to face has an aura of intimacy, of communicativeness on an intimate level. Speaking shoulder to shoulder carries the aura of shared activity, as if the two men involved were elbow-deep in some manual chore, even if both men are sitting down and doing nothing.

So, when doing a boy-friendly book group, do not set the kids facing each other and expect boys to open up. In fact, you may not want to sit them down at all. Boys, being of a more physical nature because of their brain structure, may be hindered in their access to language skills without significant stimuli. Too often when attempting to do a boy-focused book discussion we assume that after discussing the book we should engage in some activity. By then you have already lost. Do the activity, and let the discussion rise of itself.

It should be apparent that the books chosen for a book discussion group affect boys' responses to that group. We would do well to include some books that are among what I have described as "boys' literature," but that concept is general in nature. To best match the needs of your readers, allow them as much choice as possible. A middle school in Alexandria, Virginia, sponsored a monthly book club for boys only but chose books based on an "interest inventory" taken at the beginning of the school year.[10] The privately established Boys Book Club in Squamscott, Massachusetts, rotated the job of nominating books among the eight boys, not the parents who accompanied them. Each month one of the boys brought several titles to the group and the boys voted on which book they would read.[11] Such choices are important, not only to select books that actually interest the readers but to assure those readers that they have control of their own reading. If the group is coeducational, then this choice may be tempered slightly to keep a predominant point of view from dominating book choices, whether that viewpoint comes from the boys or the girls.

To really put choice in the readers' hands, we can take a cue from the free-reading assignments mentioned earlier. Just because a dozen kids are gathering to talk about books does not mean they have to all read the same book. Once or twice a year, a book group can put aside a meeting for everyone to read a book of their choice and then present that book to the group. Not only can this inspire extra reading in all the members, it may become a way of choosing the books for the coming sessions. You can also turn such a meeting into the basis of a writing project, with the group members creating reading guides for other kids.

It is also important to distance a book group, whose aim should be to promote reading for enjoyment, from a classroom discussion. Book groups should not be a way of assessing kids' reading. Sandra Lingo, who has run successful all-boys reading groups for years, warns that

> boys won't return to book club if they feel they are being compared to one another, or if there are hard questions they'll be singled out to answer. As educators, we have this nagging urge to test students to see if they have *really* read the book, but that kind of inquisition will defeat struggling readers who have taken the risk to participate in book club.[12]

In the remainder of this section I recount a few specific book discussion plans to help emphasize these general points.

Books on the Hoof

A Week in the Woods, by Andrew Clement (Aladdin, 2004), for elementary and middle school readers, and *A Walk in the Woods: Rediscovering America on the Appalachian Trail,* by Bill Bryson (Anchor, 2006), for high school readers

I was once asked to come in and save a public library book group for kids that was dying on the vine. It had never been large, had never contained any boys, and was slowly losing the members it had. The librarian asked me to turn it around. I had one meeting to work with. Against all my standard rules for such programs, I asked the parents in the community to get as many boys in as they could, by any means necessary. The results were predictable. Boys were being dragged in by their mothers and told to sit down and pay attention—this would be good for them. To make matters worse, I set up a ring of folding chairs in the middle of an empty space in the children's room. It looked like an intervention. Boys were exuding as much negative body language as they could muster, sinking down in their chairs until their shoulder blades were nearly touching the seats.

I waited, amused, until all the seats were full, then stood up, clapped my hands, and told everyone to go get their coats. There was confusion, and a little bit of disbelief, but we got everyone up and out of the library and did the entire book discussion walking through the woods. We had, of course, read Andrew Clements's *A Week in the Woods,* a book full of trail markers and nature signs. How could you possibly discuss this book sitting in a basement? And because we took the book discussion out onto the trail, the natural tendency became to discuss plot elements, not characterization. It was a huge success. Some of the boys who had refused to read the book in preparation for a book group they were being forced to attend went back later and read the book to better understand what they had experienced during the hike.

For older boys, you can do the same with Bill Bryson's *A Walk in the Woods.* The fresh air, the physicality, and the simple difference of an open-air book group appeal to a lot of boys who think such programs are constricting, confusing, and just plain boring. The idea for this booktalk came out of my experience at a special needs boarding school that specialized in extreme cases of ADHD. One of the founding principles of the school was a rejection of behavior-modifying drugs such as Ritalin. Students who arrived in September were faced with life without their meds, cold turkey, and the results were both distressing and predictable. There were many literature classes that I taught outside, on the hoof, in the early months of the school year when the students were incapable of sitting still during their withdrawal.

The Loser Olympics

Loser, by Jerry Spinelli (HarperTrophy, 2003)

Jerry Spinelli's book *Loser* is about Donald Zinkoff, a boy who is, without a doubt, a loser. This is no Disney-type ugly duckling story where the character thinks he is a loser but in the end we find a hero within. Donald Zinkoff is a loser. He wears a four-foot-tall giraffe hat to kindergarten. His handwriting is so bad it is unreadable. He idolizes his dad and wants to be a mailman just like him. He cannot play any sport to save his life, despite his unquenchable excitement to try, and fail over and over again. At his school's field day, his teacher, in an attempt at inclusion, makes Donald the anchor leg of the relay race. His team hands him a huge lead and Donald takes off running as fast as he can, arms and legs flailing, going nowhere. Every other team passes him and Donald's class comes in last. Donald Zinkoff is a loser.

What would you discuss in a book group on *Loser*? What would you ask the children?

"Was Donald Zinkoff a loser?"

The most likely reply would be, "Oh, totally. Can we have cookies now?"

Consider hosting the "Loser Olympics" for your book group, a series of events based on the book. Gather as many large boots as you can from the community, work boots, waders, galoshes, whatever will fit over a kid's shoes. Make all participants pull a pair of boots over their shoes and then run a course around the children's room in the library or down a school corridor. Be sure there are at least a few sharp curves. The kids will run like Donald Zinkoff, arms and legs flailing, and with similar results.

Next, duct-tape oven mitts over the children's hands and set them to throwing footballs to each other. Have them break into pairs and stand just inches apart. They can hand the football to each other from there. Some will still drop the ball, and those teams are eliminated. Then have each child take one step back and toss each other the ball. Keep them stepping back until only one team is left that has not fumbled itself out of the competition.

Have a writing contest next, using everybody's weak hand; watch out for the lefties who will try to use their strong hands. Print out a quotation and give it to the first player on each team to copy. That player then gives the paper to the next team member, who must copy it again, and so on, through however many teammates there are. The team whose final product is closest to the original wins the event.

There is no limit to the number of such events you can host in a Loser Olympics. Pick any scene from the book and use your imagination. The beauty of the idea is how involved each member of the book group is, and how many colorful ribbons you can give out for prizes in each event.

The Nuts and Bolts Book Club

Revenge of the Whale: The True Story of the Whaleship Essex, by Nathaniel Philbrick (Puffin, 2004)

Nathaniel Philbrick, who wrote the adult account of the sinking of the whaleship *Essex,* also wrote a children's version. *Revenge of the Whale,* a nonfiction account of the disaster that inspired *Moby-Dick,* pulls no punches, even dealing directly with the cannibalism that occurred in the attempt to reach land in escape boats. It is a powerful, exciting, edgy read. What a tragedy to lose the impact in a stale conversation about class distinctions and how the men felt about eating their shipmates. Instead, take all the chairs out of the room and put a large table there instead. Buy a cheap plastic model ship and dump the parts, the glue, and the decals in the center of the table. When the kids arrive, immediately set to work building the model. Let the conversation flow out of the activity. You may be surprised at how much more willing to talk boys are when they have something to do. The rule still stands: engage a boy's hands and the mind will follow. Pierce Howard explains the brain structure basis for this as follows:

> Male-differentiated brains . . . find it easier to handle multi-tasking, such as talking while building something. Talking, which uses the left hemisphere, doesn't interfere in a major way with building, which is visual-spatial and uses the right hemisphere. Because the female-differentiated brain handles visual-spatial tasks in both hemispheres, building and talking, which both use the left hemisphere, interfere with each other.[13]

Survivor!

The Worst-Case Scenario Survival Handbook, by Joshua Piven and David Borgenicht (Chronicle Books, 1999)

This one comes from the Shippensburg (Pennsylvania) Public Library. It comprises three components: "Live or Die," a quiz challenge based on outdoor survival techniques in the book; the "Impossible Information Hunt," a research scavenger hunt in the classic library tradition; and an "Insane Obstacle Course," adding a physical element. Competition, physicality, and library promotion all wrapped up in one program. Ideal.

PROMOTING READING TO BOYS

It is not enough to have books that appeal to boys; we must put those books in boys' hands. To do that, not only must we understand the differences between boys and girls, we must apply that knowledge to promote books in ways that speak to boys. We must allow for a certain amount of physicality in connection with reading. We must connect boys' reading with the things that matter to them. And we must lead boys to books by having those most like them— meaning men—model a love for reading.

Above all else, we must remember that many boys, especially those we most need to reach, are beginning from the assumption that reading is a solitary, sedentary, feminized activity that is closed to them. They believe that reading is boring, hard, and better suited to girls. If we fail to overcome these perceptions, we will continue to see half of our high school boys identifying themselves as nonreaders. And if they so self-identify, all of our efforts will be for naught. Overcoming these perceptions and the situations that encourage them is a job for all of us—teachers, librarians, parents, grandparents, politicians, business-people, and everyone else in our society.

Notes

1. William G. Brozo, "Bridges to Literacy for Boys," *Educational Leadership,* September 2006, 71–72.

2. Sean Cavazos-Kottke, "Five Readers Browsing: The Reading Interests of Talented Middle School Boys," *Gifted Child Quarterly,* Spring 2006, 133.

3. Sean Cavazos-Kottke, "Tuned Out but Turned On: Boys' (Dis)engaged Reading in and out of School," *Journal of Adolescent and Adult Literacy,* November 2005, 182–83.

4. Donna Lester Taylor, "'Not Just Boring Stories': Reconsidering the Gender Gap for Boys," *Journal of Adolescent and Adult Literacy,* December/January 2005, 294.

5. Shirley P. Brown and Paula Alidia Roy, "A Gender-Inclusive Approach to English/Language Arts Methods: Literacy with a Critical Lens," in *Gender in the Classroom: Foundations, Skills, Methods, and Strategies across the Curriculum,* ed. David Sadker and Ellen S. Silber (Mahwah, NJ: Erlbaum, 2007), 169.

6. Kathy Sanford, Heather Blair, and Raymond Chodzinski, "A Conversation about Boys and Literacy," *Teaching and Learning,* Spring 2007, 13.

7. Ibid., 6.

8. Lanning Taliaferro, "Education Gender Gap Leaving Boys Behind," *Journal News,* June 17, 2001, 17.

9. Ibid.

10. Randolph Mitchell, Robert M. Murphy, and Jodie M. Peters, "The Boys in Literacy Initiative: Molding Adolescent Boys into Avid Readers," *Principal,* March/April 2008, 70.

11. Julie Hahnke, "Fostering a Love of Reading," *Reporters,* December 6, 2008, A&M 7.

12. Sandra Lingo, "The All Guys Book Club: Where Boys Take the Risk to Read," *Library Media Connection,* April/May 2007, 27.

13. Pierce J. Howard, *The Owner's Manual for the Brain* (Austin, TX: Bard Press, 2006), 268.

Chapter 8

Creating the Culture of Literacy

I am often asked, if boys fail so much more often at reading, why is it that men still run the world? Why have we never had a woman president of the United States? Why are there so few women in Congress? And why are women almost unknown among the CEOs of the Fortune 500 companies? The answer is apparent within the question itself: we live in a society that does not honor reading. If we did, then those who excel at reading would be more valued. How do we convince boys to even try reading when there is no apparent connection between reading and success?

Boys read for practical reasons, but what practical reasons do they see? A jump shot can gain you millions and land you on national television, but the men who seek our highest public office make a point of hiding their intelligence because polls say they look out of touch if they appear too bookish. The men whom boys see succeeding are never seen reading. On the other hand, presidential candidates are carefully positioned to be seen throwing footballs and shooting animals. And the work of educating children is demeaned as "women's work," underpaid, and disrespected. Josephine Young theorizes, "The low correlation between school literacy success and career advancement may be one reason boys' underachievement in school literacy exists."[1]

The factors are stacked up against boys reading: they are developmentally behind girls throughout their school days; the definition of good reading is artificially skewed against the types of reading boys tend to enjoy; and boys lack role models to show them the way to reading. Given this, it is vital that we effect a shift in our culture, a shift toward putting reading at the center of our value system. We must create a culture of literacy to engulf boys and support them.

IT STARTS AT HOME

The educational world must adopt a certain amount of humility if we are to help boys become readers. We must all—teachers, school administrators, and librarians—acknowledge that children spend more time at home than they do at school. They are more influenced by the home environment than they are by the school environment. For all that we try to teach children, students will learn more in life if they become readers than they will in three years of story hour or twelve years of school. We must focus our efforts on encouraging reading as a leisure activity and on supporting parents.

Libraries that fail to acknowledge this fact are easy to spot; just look for those that bar parents and caregivers from children's programs. There is a long tradition among public librarians of asking adults to drop off children for story hour and telling them to come back in forty-five minutes. These libraries fail to see that the purpose of story hour is not to teach kids to be readers but to teach adults to be reading teachers. Story hour itself has little effect on children, coming once a week for thirty to forty weeks a year, for maybe three years of the children's lives. If reading is to become a habit, it must make its way into the culture of the home. Story hour needs to be repeated daily, year round, for most of the developmental years of the child. If this does not occur in the home, then the best efforts of the librarian will have little effect.

Libraries must invite parents and caregivers to be part of all they do with children. Librarians must model good reading, reading in volume and reading for fun, reading that is expressive and engaging, and reading that is connected to the vast experiences of the world. If story hour is the perfect reading environment for boys, then librarians must encourage others to copy their methods. Librarians, especially children's librarians, are often too content to sit within their four walls and call their work good enough without regard for the impact they make, or fail to make, in the larger community.

Parents, too, have a responsibility here. Our society has evolved to assign important tasks to specialists, and to relegate important activities to a special time and place. By doing this, we cheapen those activities. Reading is only as important as the place it finds in our calendars and day planners. We have to stop thinking of the library as a place for a pleasant diversion or, worse, a source of free babysitting. If children today see that the library is of secondary concern to their parents, then that is how they will see the library and all that goes on within it. If they see that library time is important to their parents, they will adopt that attitude. If the literacy activities that happen in the library are mirrored in the home, then those activities will be reinforced.

SCHOOL IS A GREAT PLACE TO CARE ABOUT READING

Our society embodies its beliefs about the importance of reading and learning in our schools. Schools are also the place where most local tax dollars are spent, and money is always a good indicator of what a group honors. But our schools are mired in a culture of standards. The rush to make schools somehow accountable for their success has left us with a need to measure the immeasurable. The results are predictably useless.

Although No Child Left Behind (NCLB) was promoted as a program to narrow the gap between the educations of rich and poor, minority and white students, its effect has been to broaden those gaps. The fact that poor and minority students are being doubly victimized alone should be enough to incense us as a nation against this disastrous approach. Add to that the effect this approach has on boys, and we have all the more reason to protest.

NCLB reduces school performance standards to a few high-stakes standardized tests and forces schools to show progress in every subject tested among its entire population—including its special needs students, racial and ethnic groups, and learners with limited English proficiency, if those groups are large enough in the school. If a school fails to show progress in each and every subdivision, then it is subject to increasingly harsh penalties. The contradiction inherent in this approach is apparent in the simple fact that schools with low financial support are most likely to fail, and one of the punishments is the loss of federal funds. If those federal funds, $23.5 billion of which were spent in fiscal year 2007 on NCLB programs, were used to support schools rather than to test and punish them, think of what we could do to improve the education of all students.[2]

Economic factors are just one of the causes of academic failure that are not helped a bit by testing. In 2003, the Educational Testing Service, a major beneficiary of NCLB since it produces so many of the tests, released a study that found fourteen home, school, community, and early development factors that directly mirrored gaps in achievement.[3] Even the testers understand that success on their tests depends on factors the tests themselves cannot measure or influence.

NCLB holds schools responsible for eliminating bad results but does not address the causes that underlie those results. The implication is clear: schools could do better with what they have, they just choose not to. Teachers are holding out, hurting children out of pure spite or incompetence, but the heroic politicians and bureaucrats will take care of them by dictating education policy. How do schools respond? The only way they can: they cheat.

Under NCLB, progress must be shown against arbitrary standards or schools face sanctions. Schools are not given any real help to improve performance, so the only solution is to lower the standards, as many states have done.[4] As one writer notes, "The law's perverse incentives are threatening to eliminate transparency by encouraging all states to lower standards to avoid Federal sanctions."[5] The proof is to be found in the fact that the gap between state proficiency test results and the National Assessment of Educational Progress has grown to unprecedented proportions. One simple example: 27 percent of fourth graders who passed the California reading test failed the NAEP test in 2006, up from 15 percent in 2002.[6]

Under NCLB, schools are judged on the percentage of students that pass a fixed bar of competence, not on actual progress by actual students. A school can see every student improve in their scores, but if not enough of the failing students actually move out of the failing range, then that school fails under NCLB. Another school can see every child's score drop, but if enough of the failing students actually drop out of school, then the school succeeds under NCLB. Does that suggest a strategy? Certainly. Schools have an incentive to push low-performing students to drop out, and there is ample evidence that this is happening. Linda Darling-Hammond points out that many of the steepest increases in test scores have taken place in schools with the highest dropout rates; Sharpstown High School in Houston, home of the "Texas Miracle," recently graduated a class of under three hundred that began as a freshman class of over a thousand, yet somehow the school managed to report not a single dropout.[7]

Schools also have subtler ways to lessen the chance that low-performing students will hurt the schools' test scores. One is simply to hold children back rather than promote them to a grade in which they will be tested. Since evidence shows that children held back more than once are dramatically more likely to drop out of school, this is double insurance for the school.[8] Of course, all of this ignores the good of the child.

A principal has related the story of a student held back twice in ninth grade for not passing algebra, though she passed all her other classes. She was then promoted directly to eleventh grade, bypassing the state's tenth-grade test. Unfortunately, since she lacked the tenth-grade credits she needed to graduate, she ended up dropping out anyway. She was not alone; there were 13 percent more ninth graders in this country in 2000 than there were eighth graders in 1999.[9]

Minnesota managed to get many of its schools off the "needs improvement" list by simply nullifying the existence of special needs students. Each state can set the minimum number of students it takes to make up a subgroup, so the state increased that number from twenty special needs students at a school to forty. There you go; any school with thirty special needs students no longer has to track their progress.[10] Did that move actually help any students?

Darling-Hammond points out that one of the more insidious consequences of NCLB is its denial of different learning styles. As the curriculum narrows, teachers are forced to teach one way since the students will be evaluated in only one way.[11] This hurts those with different learning styles, and one strong factor that creates differences in learning style is gender.

Indeed, for every disadvantage to poor, minority, or non-English-speaking students, there is a parallel danger for boys. All of these students are more likely to fail tests, including boys. All suffer from circumstances beyond their control, whether it is structural racism in our society, systemic poverty and the health conditions that so often accompany it, or the simple brain lag that means boys' brains do not fully catch up to girls' brains until after most of the high-stakes testing is over. If holding back students is one strategy to survive the testing regimen, remember that boys are far more likely than girls to be held back a grade. If schools are forced to encourage low-performing students to drop out of school, remember that 80 percent of those dropouts are likely to be male. NCLB may unfairly hurt the very students it proposes to help, and it does just as much damage to one at-risk group it wholly ignores: boys.

RAISE THE CRY

How much energy has gone into satisfying the recent cultural need for standards? Energy that could be put to better use. Perhaps the most tragic side of the NCLB testing fiasco is how counterproductive our efforts have been. Schools have dropped all pretense of promoting reading and learning as lifelong activities in favor of preparing children to take a series of tests that supposedly measure the children's success at reading and learning. If we were actually to make children better readers, then we would expect them to do better on the tests. Still, we do not focus on promoting reading in volume, the one factor proven to create better readers. The reason is simple: schools know that the tests measure skills only partially related to reading, so they focus on those skills—to the detriment of children—because that is the only way to keep from losing even more control if some oversight agency decides the school is not showing adequate improvement.

We have put schools in an impossible position, and the schools' reactions have been predictable. As the old jest goes, the great national oxymoron is military intelligence. Well, we have now found a greater one: national education policy. There is no way to dictate to schools across the country anything that will help an individual student learn. Indeed, for the student who struggles, national dictates take away the only hope he has, that a teacher will see his struggles and tailor a solution to him. The tragedy of NCLB is that it is designed to ensure children do get left behind. The parent of every struggling learner, especially those who struggle at reading, should be outraged.

And there is both the heart of the problem and the beginnings of a solution. NCLB, all the attendant legislation at the national and state level, and all the prepackaged reading programs proliferating in our schools to address this legislation survive for the simple reason that the great mass of parents support them, or at least do not object to them. Parents hear horror stories about bad teachers and bad schools, and they demand accountability without considering the implications of that demand. Forcing onto a system a form of measurement does not ensure that the measurements are meaningful.

No national score can ever help a child read or learn. If we want to save children, especially those who fail at reading, then we must return as much control as possible to the frontline teachers in the classroom. Teachers must be able to make adjustments for the good of individual students, free from dictates from Washington, their state capital, the district, and even their principals. Does this mean that some bad teachers will be able to continue to teach badly? Absolutely, but this argument is a red herring. The vast majority of teachers are hardworking, competent, and interested in the success of their students. Every one of those good teachers is hurt by efforts to hold a few bad ones accountable.

It would be more effective to let the good teachers teach. Good teachers value reading as a lifelong passion and transfer that value to the children they teach. That is how you build a culture of literacy. Honoring only the percentage of correct answers a child can produce on a test of trivial questions can produce only a culture of standards.

WHAT SCHOOLS SHOULD DO

Give schools the chance, and they can make many changes to create an overarching atmosphere that honors literacy. Schools must adopt the ideal that everybody is a reading teacher. Having a reading specialist is fine, but it tends to create the idea—among parents, faculty, and the kids themselves—that the job of teaching reading is safely in the hands of an expert and need not be considered further. If reading is something that can be handled by one person, or one department, then it cannot be all that important. Principals need to know that their primary job is to promote reading. Science teachers need to know that students learn more about science by reading than they ever learn in the lab. Custodians in our schools must see that they have a role in turning all the students in their care into readers. Teaching reading is everybody's job.

Schools have answered this challenge with "Drop Everything and Read" programs. A time is set aside when everyone in the school, from students to principals to lunchroom workers, stops what they are doing and reads. Even better, some schools impose these moments at random. The announcement goes out over the school intercom and all else stops. What a message this must send to the students in these schools: reading can occur anytime, anywhere, and nothing is more important.

Schools can go further with this cultural shift by putting the school library in its proper place at the center of school life. Many schools pay lip service to this concept by putting the library in the physical center of new school buildings, but too often our actions belie these good intentions. Schools that cut library staff or eliminate qualifications in order to use less-trained aides instead of trained librarians are doing nothing to promote the place of reading within their schools. Tying up what little time librarians have with students with non-reading-related activities is equally harmful. Reading time with librarians is sacrificed to technology time, study hours, and mere crowd control.

Schools need to prepare children for the technology they face in the real world, granted, but too many schools just assume that the time, space, and resources they require to teach technology must come at the expense of traditional library instruction. The result is schedules that replace library time with computer time, libraries split in half to put in computer rooms, and library collections decimated to save money for new technology. Few schools would cut the science curriculum in half to teach keyboarding; why do we accept that fate for school libraries? Alison Follos asserts that "underutilizing the school library's collection is the glaring weak link to developing a literature-enriched curriculum."[12]

READING IS EVERYONE'S JOB

Ultimately, the job of turning boys into readers is too large to be accomplished by schools and libraries alone. It takes a culture that immerses boys in literacy. And creating that culture requires more than change within libraries, schools, and even children's homes. We must all create an environment where boys feel supported in their reading, and where reading itself is held up as a cultural value.

"Boys Booked on Barbershops" is a program that seeks to produce just such a society. Formed in 2004 as part of the fifteenth annual African American Read-In Chain, this program seeks to place books of high interest to boys, especially boys of color, in barbershops.[13] The shops' responsibility is to create a nook where boys can encounter books while they wait for their haircuts, and where adults can read to them. The obvious genius of this program is that it brings literacy into one of the most universal of all male experiences. The auxiliary value is in how many authors, athletes, businessmen, and others it connects with to surround boys with literacy. These book nooks enable opportunities for celebrations, read-ins, photo opportunities, and the like throughout the year. The fact that Boys Booked on Barbershops has a companion program for girls, known as Girls Booked on Beautyshops, just highlights how completely this initiative understands the issues at hand. Creating a literacy-supportive environment means ensuring that all members are readers.

If there is one place to get inspired about surrounding boys with literacy, that place is the U.S. Marine Corps. Here, where many would be stunned to discover that reading is honored, we find a world where advancement is tied to reading. The Marine Corps has a reading list of required titles for each level of rank. It is heavy on the nonfiction, strongly tilted to war stories, and sprinkled with the likes of Orson Scott Card and C. S. Forester. Although women are a part of the Marine Corps, here is the apex of traditional boy culture, and at its center is a reading list.[14] Not only are marines expected to read, and read throughout their careers, but the commandant of the Marine Corps himself has ordered all commanders to "view the professional development of their subordinates as a direct responsibility of their performance as commanders, and to develop local programs that emphasize reading and self-directed study."[15]

In *Leatherneck*, the Marine Corp publication, Major S. D. Griffin writes, "Every Marine needs both education and training. The further you go in the Corps, the more responsibility you accept for the education and training of those you lead."[16] Everyone reads, and being a leader means teaching reading. That is culture in support of literacy. The U.S. Navy, too, has a reading program—one that features military strategy, management, leadership, cultural awareness, and a little Robert A. Heinlein.[17]

TEACHERS AND LIBRARIANS NEED SUPPORT, TOO

Asking those responsible for promoting reading to do their jobs without the support of the community will fail, because they will lack the authority to do the work and because it will not be possible to continue to attract excellent talent to those jobs. Teachers and librarians cannot do this job on their own, but neither can we do this job without great talent and energy in these positions.

The issue of teachers' pay has long been in the public debate. We entrust our children to these people and pay them less than those to whom we entrust our pets and our cars. Maybe that is why it is so easy to take away their autonomy within the classroom. How much can we trust people we pay so little? It is a circular argument that endangers the future of our educational system. The best of the best may someday decide that the pet care industry is more appealing than education, and people are less likely to sue them for correcting the behavior of a cocker spaniel.

Public library children's librarians are the true reading specialists in most communities, and the fact that we pay them on a feminized pay scale should not change that fact. What we pay children's librarians, even on the depressed scale of what we pay librarians in general, is testimony to how little even librarians honor the importance of reading. In 1997, the average beginning salary for a graduate of a master's program in library science in the United States was $30,270. For those who went into services for youth, the average was $27,896, or 7.8 percent less than the average.[18] By 2005, that gap had risen to 8.4 percent.[19] Factoring out differences in education and experience, we pay librarians who work with children less than we pay other librarians, and the gap is widening. How can we say we honor reading, even in the literary havens that are our public libraries, if those who are most responsible for promoting reading are so little honored?

READING ALONE

Our society should heed the warning in Robert D. Putnam's book *Bowling Alone: The Collapse and Revival of American Community* (Simon and Schuster, 2000). Putnam points out that so much of what was once engaged in, and thus honored, as a society we now engage in behind the closed doors of our own homes. Social value must be exercised communally.

But we cannot be content to read socially as we always have. Recent attempts at advocating "One Book, One Community" have sought to establish a communal reading value but have done so largely by projecting our traditional book groups onto a new scale. It will take more than that. Our book groups have long proved to be more appealing to women than to men. We need to celebrate reading as a self-directed activity, even when done in consort with others.

Groups that engage boys need to be active in including literacy in all that they do. Little Leagues should promote baseball books and host authors at their celebrations. Boy Scouts should have a literary magazine of boys writing for boys.

Those who promote the best in reading need to take into account the different point of view that so many boys have. The Newbery Committee especially, but also the committees that choose the Printz Award for teenagers, the Hornbook Award, the Coretta Scott King Award, and the National Book Award among so many others, should take a hard look within. They need to see that they speak for all readers, not just the ones that look and think like they do. All of these awards have fallen into somewhat biased assessment, the Newbery Committee most notably so. It is time to recognize that quality exists in many forms, in many genres, and in books that speak to boys.

We as a society should contemplate the story told in Daniel Pennac's superb little memoir of an educator's experience, *Better Than Life*. Pennac tells of a college professor, teaching a class of advanced literature students, who had the audacity to read to college students in his class. If these were going to be educated people, then there were some books to which they should be exposed. Pennac goes on to describe the incredible effect the same approach had on teenagers who considered themselves too cool for school and were considered lost cases. He shows us a glimpse of what a world that honors reading might look like. He also gives his "Reader's Bill of Rights":

1. The right not to read.
2. The right to skip pages.
3. The right to not finish a book.
4. The right to reread.
5. The right to read anything.
6. The right to escapism.
7. The right to read anywhere.
8. The right to browse.
9. The right to read out loud.
10. The right to not defend your tastes.[20]

These are not rights we need to preserve for ourselves, Pennac argues; we do that anyway. These are the rights we need to preserve for children. In a time when personal political rights are under assault, what chance do we have of defending personal intellectual rights? When our culture is splintering, can we create a culture of literacy to help all of us, boys included, to reach our full potential as human beings? A generation of boys await that answer.

Read Like a Warrior: Books from the Navy and Marine Book Lists

Ambrose, Stephen E. *Band of Brothers: E Company, 506th Regiment, 101st Airborne from Normandy to Hitler's Eagle's Nest.* Simon and Schuster, 2001.

Bradley, James. *Flags of Our Fathers.* Bantam, 2006.

Card, Orson Scott. *Ender's Game.* Tor, 2006.

Forester, C. S. *Rifleman Dodd.* Nautical and Aviation Publishing Company of America, 1990.

Heinlein, Robert A. *Starship Troopers.* Ace, 1987.

Hirsch, James S. *Two Souls Indivisible: The Friendship That Saved Two POWs in Vietnam.* Mariner Books, 2005.

Hornfischer, James D. *Last Stand of the Tin Can Sailors: The Extraordinary World War II Story of the U.S. Navy's Finest Hour.* Bantam, 2005.

Krulak, Lt. Gen. Victor H. *First to Fight: An Inside View of the U.S. Marine Corps.* U.S. Naval Institute Press, 1999.

McPherson, James M. *Battle Cry of Freedom: The Civil War Era.* Oxford University Press, 2003.

O'Brian, Patrick. *Master and Commander.* Norton, 1994.

Stillwell, Paul, ed. *Golden Thirteen: Recollections of the First Black Naval Officers.* U.S. Naval Institute Press, 2003.

Sun Tzu. *The Art of War.* Shambhala, 2005.

Twining, Merrill B. *No Bended Knee: The Battle for Guadalcanal.* Presidio Press, 2004.

Webb, James. *Fields of Fire.* Bantam, 2001.

Wouk, Herman. *The Caine Mutiny.* Back Bay Books, 2002.

Books on Reading, Culture, and the Culture of Literacy

Meier, Deborah, et al. *Many Children Left Behind: How the No Child Left Behind Act Is Damaging Our Children and Our Schools.* Beacon Press, 2004.

Pennac, Daniel. *Better Than Life.* Coach House Press, 1994.

Putnam, Robert D. *Bowling Alone: The Collapse and Revival of American Community.* Simon and Schuster, 2000.

Notes

1. Josephine Peyton Young and William G. Brozo, "Boys Will Be Boys, or Will They? Literacy and Masculinities," *Reading Research Quarterly,* July/August/September 2001, 319.

2. Dan Lips, "Giving NCLB an A-PLUS Boost," *USA Today,* January 2008, 66.

3. Deborah Meier et al., *Many Children Left Behind: How the No Child Left Behind Act Is Damaging Our Children and Our Schools* (Boston: Beacon Press, 2004), 61.

4. Ibid., 16.

5. Lips, "Giving NCLB an A-PLUS Boost," 67.

6. Lynn Olson, "Gaps in Proficiency Levels on State Tests and NAEP Found to Grow," *Education Week,* April 18, 2007, 12.

7. Meier et al., *Many Children Left Behind,* 21.

8. Ibid., 37.

9. Ibid., 38, 94.

10. Ibid., 55–56.

11. Ibid., 18.

12. Alison M. G. Follos, *Reviving Reading: School Library Programming, Author Visits and Books That Rock!* (Westport, CT: Libraries Unlimited, 2006), 13.

13. Sabrina A. Brinson, "Boys Booked on Barbershops: A Cutting-Edge Literacy Program," *Young Children,* March, 2007, 42–48.

14. U.S. Marine Corps, *Professional Reading Program Reading List,* www.mcu.usmc.mil/ProDev/ProfReadingPgm.htm.

15. U.S. Marine Corps, ALMAR 030/07, Memo on Marine Corps Professional Reading Program, www.mcu.usmc.mil/ProDev/reading%20files/AlMar%20030%2007.pdf.

16. S. D. Griffin, "Read a Book, Get Ahead," *Leatherneck,* December 2007, 44.

17. "Navy Reading: Accelerate Your Mind," www.navyreading.navy.mil.

18. Virginia A. Walter, *Children and Libraries: Getting It Right* (Chicago: American Library Association, 2001), 41.

19. Stephanie Maatta, "Closing the Gap," *Library Journal,* October 15, 2005, 30.

20. Daniel Pennac, *Better Than Life* (Toronto: Coach House Press, 1994), 170–71.

Conclusion

Boys and Reading— What the Future Holds

What does the future hold for boys and reading? All attempts at peering into the future are hazardous at best, but we can consider some trends and some realities. Both entail facing some hard challenges; that is what is so daunting about looking ahead. Both can be changed; that is what is so encouraging about looking ahead.

We too often approach the reading gap among boys as a problem of illiteracy. It is not. Boys are falling victim to an epidemic of *aliteracy,* having the ability to read and no compulsion whatsoever to do so. The consequence of this misperception is clear: the gap between boys' and girls' success in reading is getting wider. Fourth-grade girls have long scored higher in reading than boys, but according to the National Assessment of Educational Progress, that gap increased between 1998 and 2000.[1] A U.S. Department of Education report in 2005 showed that the reading and writing gaps among high school students widened between 1992 and 2002.[2] These are just a few of the indicators that show boys falling further behind girls. True, some indicators show that in absolute terms boys may be making some progress in some areas, but the need for literacy skills continues to rise in our increasingly complex society and increasingly high-tech economy. Staying put, while others move forward, could land too many of our boys with only one option, that involving paper hats and cash registers with pictures of food on them. We must offer them more.

Many of our schools are making valiant efforts to reverse this trend. Well trained over the past two decades in different intelligences, leading to different learning styles, many teachers have made a good-faith effort to include what is called *differentiated instruction* in their classrooms. Differentiated instruction means teaching with an eye toward these different learning styles. Teachers who have adopted these methods should be roundly praised; they are taking on a great deal more work than they need to just to give some of the underperforming students a fighting chance. The number of teachers who take on this challenge tells me that so many of them really do care about boys and are willing to do something about it.

Slower to be adopted, but there on the horizon, is *differentiated assessment*. This next step would mean that we not only teach students in ways that speak to them but assess their progress by allowing them to demonstrate their achievement in ways that flow from their particular learning styles. I believe that this focus on differences is a direct result of the Girl Power movement, and one more gift to come from that productive chapter in our history. If different intelligences, differentiated instruction, and differentiated assessment were really to take root in our schools, boys would benefit immeasurably.

And therein lies the rub. The benefit would be difficult to measure. Differentiated assessment is hard to put on a statewide or national chart for some politician to pose beside. In management terms, if something cannot be measured, then it did not happen, and contemporary education policy is all about corporate-style management. Schools today are forced to prove they are effective, even if that effort means they cannot get anything done. George Wood, a high school principal, writes, "What NCLB (No Child Left Behind) leaves behind . . . is the notion that schools have any role aside from preparing our children to take tests."[3] The standardization of classroom instruction for the sake of assessing all students with the same narrow vehicle has all but destroyed two decades of progress toward differentiated instruction and any hope of ever seeing differentiated assessment. For so many boys who have proved to be unsuccessful under the most generalized of school approaches, this means that schools hold little hope for their future.

If schools are to be a hope for boys in the future, there is a simple task that we as a society must complete. Think of it as a great quest in one of those fantasy stories boys love so much. We need to repeal No Child Left Behind and dismantle both the systems and the theories that made its existence possible. Every teacher, every librarian, every parent, every businessperson who ever wants a competent workforce, every citizen who values fairness and justice in our society, and every politician who can still talk about public service with a straight face needs to stand up today and pledge, publicly, their opposition to this federally mandated tyranny of standards. We need to say clearly that the use of high-sounding terms, and the argument that this legislation is for the good of those it will ultimately harm, is a cynical play on the apathy and credulity of the American people, and we will not stand for it.

No prescription from Washington will help children learn. If the federal government is going to fund schools, then it should do so freely with no strings attached. Replace the nine hundred or so pages of the No Child Left Behind legislation with a single line: "The federal government will allocate to every school district $3,000 per year per pupil enrolled, adjusted for inflation, from this point forward." No strings, no mandates. Yes, I readily acknowledge that money does not solve problems, but the lack of money has certainly caused them. There are school districts that cannot educate children because they do not have the resources. These districts may know what they need to do, but instead they are forced to do things they know will not help, things that may indeed hurt their students, just to get the money they need to stay open.

If the federal government cannot see its way clear to support these schools without strings, then it should stay out of the education business altogether and lessen the tax burdens on states and municipalities so they can raise more resources locally. The only thing that will improve education for struggling students—and that includes boys—is the support and freedom that individual teachers have within their classrooms. Does that mean allowing some bad teachers to teach badly? Absolutely, but that number is minuscule compared to the number of caring, dedicated teachers who would teach better if we just gave them the resources and the opportunities.

THE ROLE OF RESEARCH

The research community is by and large on the side of hope. Brain studies and education research have bent their lenses on gender differences in the past decade, producing a more dispassionate and realistic picture of the real differences between boys and girls and how we can use that knowledge to better serve both. There are still those who fear that acknowledging innate differences between the genders feeds sexism. This view is nourished by a history of ill-used science that equated "different" with "superior" in a warped zero-sum game that has victimized girls, minorities, and the poor. Granted—but the advance of good science has lessened these objections, and I believe it will continue to do so.

We who use this research must be ever vigilant that our words and actions do not give credence to these fears. We must be sure that our efforts to help boys do not amount to blaming feminists or harming girls. There are those among the loudest of advocates for boys who equate the two, and they must be disavowed constantly and consistently. If we are to create a culture of literacy, which I see as the only long-term solution to the boys' reading problem, then everyone must be involved, and everyone's reading supported.

THE FUTURE OF BOYS' LITERATURE

If there is one trend that is truly encouraging, it is in the availability of great books for boys. The difference between what is available now and what was available when I was a boy is astonishing. Writers such as Jon Scieszka, Gordon Korman, Todd Strasser, Joseph Bruchac, and so many others have created an incredible body of work that speaks to a large number of boys. The quality of that literature continues to improve as well. Too often in the past, boys were drawn to lesser works because they were the only books that made an attempt to reach boys.

Nowadays, one can look at gothic horror and find Darren Shan, whose works are more compelling than those of R. L. Stine were less than a generation ago when he was breaking new ground for boys. Matt Christopher, once virtually the only option for sports books aimed at elementary students, has been superseded by the superior works of Mike Lupica and John Feinstein. Boys' literature has always been stigmatized as being of lesser quality, partly because we do not respect its forms. Now it is harder to make that assertion, since the quality of the writing itself is improving in absolute terms. Perhaps some day Dav Pilkey's work will be recognized for what it is: proto-fantasy. *Captain Underpants* contains all the themes and forms of true fantasy, in a package that is accessible to those who are not ready for Tolkien, at least not yet.

We are a long way, though, from seriously honoring boys' literature. At best, the books that appeal to so many boys, especially those boys who fail to connect with the reading foisted upon them by adults, have gained a measure of grudging acceptance. Until more of this literature appears on summer reading lists, on book award lists, and even in school curriculums, boys will consider themselves bad readers, even those boys who do read. What other conclusion can they come to if everything presented as good reading has no appeal to them?

Adult writers may help bring acceptance to boys' literature by writing genre books that appeal to children and teens. James Patterson has done this with his Maximum Ride series, and so have Ridley Pearson, John Grisham, and Robert Parker. Boys have long skipped the reading that adults have earmarked for them and gone straight to the adult shelves for Stephen King, Orson Scott Card, and the like. Now the adult shelves are coming to them. We can only hope that less pigeonholing of authors will allow more boys the thrill of reading that so many in past generations experienced only when they got out of high school.

THE CANARIES IN THE COAL MINE

We often think of the phrase "canary in the coal mine" as a portent of danger. When the canary stops singing, you know there is trouble afoot. We can see this symbolism strikingly when it comes to boys and reading. In that case, the canaries have been suffocating for generations. The fact that boys have struggled to read for so long leads us to wonder what the atmosphere has been like for everybody else. The realizations of the 1970s and 1980s about girls' lack of success in math and science, emotional vulnerability in our schools, and ultimate failure to take advantage of college opportunities left us wondering what our society was doing to girls. And though we made great strides toward solving many of these problems, we had yet to address the underlying issues that allowed us, as a society, to tolerate systemic inequalities in opportunity.

What we had was a mass psychological insecurity. We had left unresolved the war on poverty. We had accepted legal gains in the rights of minorities without social equality. We faced immigration issues without being able to reconcile expedience with our purported values as a nation. In the face of all this inequality, piled on top of the unfinished work we had toward eliminating the barriers toward success for girls, how could we possibly take seriously the petty issue of boys and reading?

As usual, the answer lies embedded in the question. How can we take seriously the issue of boys and reading? Because it seriously matters. Making it a question of whose pain is greater, about which injustice is more abhorrent, just perpetuates the idea that inequalities are acceptable, just so long as we take care of the bad ones. That thinking once left us with Jim Crow laws.

Boys and reading is not a problem on par with racial violence, crushing poverty, or the fact that women get paid less than men for doing the same work. It just means that large numbers of our boys will never reach their economic or personal potential. And if we cannot address a problem as clear as this, how do we begin to muster the courage to face the other issues in our society? We as a culture must make a stand that everyone is worthy of a chance to reach his or her potential. If we can make a few basic changes, if we can offer the life of a reader to all our children, including boys, then maybe our next generation will have the literacy tools to engage even bigger problems.

The canary was not the most important issue in the coal mine. Ultimately, it was hard to care a great deal about its fate. But a singing canary meant a healthy mine, just as much as a quiet one meant danger. Seeing reading as valued by our boys would be a clear sign that the atmosphere in our society is getting better.

Can we get enough air into the mines to wake up the canaries? Before I die, I'd like to hear those canaries sing. How about you?

Notes

1. Lucille Renwick, "What's the Buzz?" *Instructor,* August 2001, 8.

2. Richard Whitmire, "Boy Trouble," *New Republic,* January 23, 2006, 15.

3. Deborah Meier et al., *Many Children Left Behind: How the No Child Left Behind Act Is Damaging Our Children and Our Schools* (Boston: Beacon Press, 2004), 34.

Bibliography

Alexander, Gabriel. "CUSD Looks to Close Reading, Math Gap between Boys, Girls." *Clovis Independent,* June 9, 2006, 1.

Allen, Jennifer. "My Literary Lunches with Boys." *Educational Leadership,* September 2006, 67–70.

American Association of University Women Education Foundation. *How Schools Shortchange Girls.* Annapolis Junction, MD: American Association of University Women, 1992.

Aronson, Marc. "Boys: Defective Girls." *School Library Journal,* January 2007, 32.

Austin, Liz. "More U.S. Schools Segregating Sexes." *Associated Press,* August 24, 2004.

Blackburn, Mollie V. "Boys and Literacies: What Difference Does Gender Make?" *Reading Research Quarterly,* April/May/June 2003, 276–87.

Bloom, Adi. "Girls Go for Little Women but Boys Prefer Lara." *Times Educational Supplement,* March 15, 2002, 18.

Brinson, Sabrina A. "Boys Booked on Barbershops: A Cutting-Edge Literacy Program." *Young Children,* March 2007, 42–48.

Brown, Shirley P., and Paula Alidia Roy. "A Gender-Inclusive Approach to English/Language Arts Methods: Literacy with a Critical Lens." In *Gender in the Classroom: Foundations, Skills, Methods, and Strategies across the Curriculum,* ed. David Sadker and Ellen S. Silber. Mahwah, NJ: Erlbaum, 2007.

Brozo, William G. "Bridges to Literacy for Boys." *Educational Leadership,* September 2006, 71–74.

———. "Gender and Reading Literacy." *Reading Today,* February/March 2005, 18.

———. *To Be a Boy, To Be a Reader.* Newark, DE: International Reading Association, 2002.

Cart, Michael. "What about Boys?" *Booklist,* January 1 and January 15, 2000, 892.

Cavazos-Kottke, Sean. "Five Readers Browsing: The Reading Interests of Talented Middle School Boys." *Gifted Child Quarterly,* Spring 2006, 132–47.

———. "Tuned Out but Turned On: Boys' (Dis)engaged Reading in and out of School." *Journal of Adolescent and Adult Literacy,* November 2005, 180–83.

Clark, Christina, and Kate Rumbold. *Reading for Pleasure: A Research Overview.* National Literacy Trust, 2006.

Clavel, Matthew. "Save the Males: A Case for Making Schools Friendlier to Boys." *American Enterprise,* July/August 2005, 30–32.

"College Degree Gender Gap." *Vocational Training News,* July 18, 2002, 4.

Costello, Bill. "Leveraging Gender Differences to Boost Test Scores." *Principal,* January/February 2008, 48–52.

Cox, Adam J. *Boys of Few Words: Raising Our Sons to Communicate and Connect.* New York: Guilford Press, 2006.

Dahlhauser, Julie. "Motivating Boys as Beginning Readers." *Teacher Librarian,* February 2003, 29–31.

Dillon, Karen. "No Girls Allowed: Men Bond over Books." *Roanoke Times,* August 3, 2007, C1.

Doiron, Ray. "Boy Books, Girl Books." *Teacher Librarian,* February 2003, 14–16.

"Educators Keep an Eye on Boys-Only Experiment at Thornton Academy." *Associated Press,* February 10, 2008.

Elias, Marilyn. "Electronic World Swallows Up Kids' Time, Study Finds." *USA Today,* March 10, 2005, A1.

Fields, Cheryl. "Summers on Women in Science." *Change,* May/June 2005, 8–10.

Fine, Jon. "Where the Boys Aren't." *BusinessWeek,* November 7, 2005, 24.

Fine, Sean. "Schools Told to Fix Boys' Low Grades." *Globe and Mail,* August 27, 2001, http://globeandmail.com/series/school/fix.html.

Flannery, Mary Ellen. "No Girls Allowed." *NEA Today,* 2006, www.nea.org/neatoday/0604/singlesex.html.

Follos, Alison M. G. *Reviving Reading: School Library Programming, Author Visits and Books That Rock!* Westport, CT: Libraries Unlimited, 2006.

Fulghum, Robert. *It Was on Fire When I Lay Down on It.* New York: Villard, 1989.

Gray, John. *Men Are from Mars, Women Are from Venus.* New York: HarperCollins, 1992.

Griffin, S. D. "Read a Book, Get Ahead." *Leatherneck,* December 2007, 42–44.

Gurian, Michael. *Boys and Girls Learn Differently! A Guide for Teachers and Parents.* San Francisco: Jossey-Bass, 2002.

Guys Read Pilot Program: Final Report. Fairbanks North Star Borough Public Library, 2007.

Hahnke, Julie. "Fostering a Love of Reading." *Reporters,* December 6, 2008, A&M 7.

Hannaford, Carla. *Smart Moves: Why Learning Is Not All in Your Head.* Arlington, VA: Great Ocean Publishers, 1995.

Hefner, David. "Where the Boys Aren't." *Black Issues in Higher Education,* June 17, 2004, 70–75.

Howard, Pierce J. *The Owner's Manual for the Brain.* Austin, TX: Bard Press, 2006.

Howe, James. *Screaming Mummies of the Pharaoh's Tomb II.* New York: Atheneum Books for Young Readers, 2003.

Ingles, Steven J., et al. *A Profile of the American Sophomore in 2002: Initial Results from the Base Year of the Education Longitudinal Study of 2002.* Washington, DC: National Center for Education Statistics, 2005.

Jones, Patrick, and Dawn Cartwright Fiorelli. "Overcoming the Obstacle Course: Teenage Boys and Reading." *Teacher Librarian,* February 2003, 9–13.

Katusic, Slavica K., et al. "Incidence of Reading Disability in a Population-Based Birth Cohort, 1976–1982, Rochester, Minn." *Mayo Clinic Proceedings,* November 2001, 1081–92.

Kenney, Brian. "Is There Really a (Boy) Problem?" *School Library Journal,* September 1, 2007, 11.

Kimura, Doreen. "Sex Differences in the Brain." *Scientific American,* September 1992, 118–25.

Kindlon, Dan, and Michael Thompson. *Raising Cain: Protecting the Emotional Life of Boys.* New York: Ballantine, 2000.

Kipnis, Adam. *Angry Young Men: How Parents, Teachers and Counselors Can Help "Bad Boys" Become Good Men.* San Francisco: Jossey-Bass, 2002.

Kokur, Kevin. "Turning Boys into Readers." *Casper Star Tribune,* July 31, 2007, C1–C2.

Krashen, Stephen. *The Power of Reading.* Westport, CT: Libraries Unlimited, 2004.

Lingo, Sandra. "The All Guys Book Club: Where Boys Take the Risk to Read." *Library Media Connection,* April/May 2007, 24–28.

Lips, Dan. "Giving NCLB an A-PLUS Boost." *USA Today,* January 2008, 66–68.

Maatta, Stephanie. "Closing the Gap." *Library Journal,* October 15, 2005, 30.

Maughan, Barbara, Richard Rowe, Rolf Loeber, and Magda Stouthamer-Loeber. "Reading Problems and Depressed Mood." *Journal of Abnormal Child Psychology,* April 2003, 219–29.

Mead, Sara. *The Evidence Suggests Otherwise: The Truth about Boys and Girls.* Washington, DC: Education Sector, 2006.

Meier, Deborah, et al. *Many Children Left Behind: How the No Child Left Behind Act Is Damaging Our Children and Our Schools.* Boston: Beacon Press, 2004.

Mitchell, Randolph, Robert M. Murphy, and Jodie M. Peters. "The Boys in Literacy Initiative: Molding Adolescent Boys into Avid Readers." *Principal,* March/April 2008, 70–71.

Morley, Judith A., and Sandra E. Russell. "Making Literature Meaningful: A Classroom/Library Partnership." In *Battling Dragons: Issues and Controversy in Children's Literature,* by Susan Lehr. Portsmouth, NH: Heinemann, 1995.

National Center for Education Statistics, Institute of Educational Sciences. *Digest of Educational Statistics 2007.* Washington, DC: U.S. Department of Education, 2008.

"Navy Reading: Accelerate Your Mind." www.navyreading.navy.mil.

"Newsmaker: Jon Scieszka." *American Libraries,* May 2008, 31.

Olson, Lynn. "Gaps in Proficiency Levels on State Tests and NAEP Found to Grow." *Education Week,* April 18, 2007, 12.

Pennac, Daniel. *Better Than Life.* Toronto: Coach House Press, 1994.

Phillips, Angela. *The Trouble with Boys.* New York: Basic Books, 1994.

Pirie, Bruce. *Teenage Boys and High School English.* Portsmouth, NH: Heinemann, 2002.

Pollack, William. *Real Boys: Rescuing Our Sons from the Myths of Boyhood.* New York: Random House, 1998.

Pomerantz, Eva M., Ellen Rydell Altermatt, and Jill L. Saxon. "Making the Grade but Feeling Distressed: Gender Differences in Academic Performance and Internal Distress." *Journal of Educational Psychology,* June 2002, 396–404.

Pottorff, Donald D., Deborah Phelps-Zientarski, and Michelle E. Skovera. "Gender Perceptions of Elementary and Middle School Students about Literacy at Home and School." *Journal of Research and Development in Education,* Summer 1996, 203–11.

Renwick, Lucille. "What's the Buzz?" *Instructor,* August 2001, 8.

Ripley, Amanda. "Who Says a Woman Can't Be Einstein?" *Time,* March 7, 2005, 55.

Rivers, Caryl, and Rosalind Chait Barnett. "The Myth of 'The Boy Crisis.'" *Washington Post,* April 9, 2006, B01.

Robinson, Christine. "Boys: A Developmental Difference." *Casper Star Tribune,* August 1, 2007, A1–A5.

Royer, James M., and Rachel E. Wing. "Making Sense of Sex Differences in Reading and Math Assessment: The Practice and Engagement Hypothesis." *Issues in Education,* 2002, 77–86.

Sadker, David, and Ellen S. Silber, eds. *Gender in the Classroom: Foundations, Skills, Methods, and Strategies across the Curriculum.* Mahwah, NJ: Erlbaum, 2007.

Sanford, Kathy. "Gendered Literacy Experiences: The Effects of Expectation and Opportunity for Boys' and Girls' Learning." *Journal of Adolescent and Adult Literacy,* December 2005/January 2006, 302–15.

Sanford, Kathy, Heather Blair, and Raymond Chodzinski. "A Conversation about Boys and Literacy." *Teaching and Learning,* Spring 2007, 4–14.

Sax, Leonard. *Why Gender Matters: What Parents and Teachers Need to Know about the Emerging Science of Sex Differences.* New York: Doubleday, 2005.

———. "The Boy Problem." *School Library Journal,* September 2007, 40–43.

Schneider, Helen. "My Child and ADHD: Chances of Being Diagnosed." *Pediatrics for Parents,* September 2007, 9–11.

"School Experiments with Same-Sex Reading Groups." *Curriculum Review,* April 2005, 8.

Scieszka, Jon. "Guys and Reading." *Teacher Librarian,* February 2003, 17–18.

"Secondary Schools Get Free Books to Boost Reading among Teenage Boys." *M2PressWIRE,* May 16, 2007.

Shallcross, Lynne. "Girl Power." *ASEE Prism,* February 2007, 30–33.

Skarbrevik, Karl J. "Gender Differences among Students Found Eligible for Special Education." *European Journal of Special Needs Education,* June 2002, 97–107.

Smith, Michael W., and Jeffrey D. Wilhelm. *Reading Don't Fix No Chevys: Literacy in the Lives of Young Men.* Portsmouth, NH: Heinemann, 2002.

Sommers, Christina Hoff. *The War against Boys.* New York: Simon and Schuster, 2000.

Steiner, Stan. "Where Have All the Men Gone? Male Role Models in the Reading Crisis." *PNLA Quarterly,* Summer 2000, 17.

Strauss, Valerie. "Educators Differ on Why Boys Lag in Reading." *Washington Post,* March 15, 2005, A12.

Sullivan, Michael. *Connecting Boys with Books: What Libraries Can Do.* Chicago: American Library Association, 2003.

Taliaferro, Lanning. "Education Gender Gap Leaving Boys Behind." *Journal News,* June 17, 2001, 17.

Taylor, Donna Lester. "'Not Just Boring Stories': Reconsidering the Gender Gap for Boys." *Journal of Adolescent and Adult Literacy,* December/January 2005, 290–98.

Toppo, Greg. "Funny, but Boys Do Read." *USA Today,* July 6, 2005, Life, 8d.

Trzesniewski, Kali, et al. "Revisiting the Association between Reading Achievement and Antisocial Behavior: New Evidence of an Environmental Explanation from a Twin Study." *Child Development,* January/February 2006, 72–88.

Tunnell, Michael O., and James S. Jacobs. "Series Fiction and Young Readers." *Booklist,* September 15, 2005, 64–65.

U.S. Marine Corps. "Professional Reading Program Reading List." www.mcu. usmc.mil/ProDev/ProfReadingPgm.htm.

———. ALMAR 030/07. Memo on Marine Corps Professional Reading Program. www.mcu.usmc.mil/ProDev/reading%20files/AlMar%20 030%2007.pdf.

Vogel, Susan A. "Gender Differences in Intelligence, Language, Visual-Motor Abilities, and Academic Achievement in Students with Learning Disabilities: A Review of the Literature." *Journal of Learning Disabilities,* January, 1990, 44–52.

Walter, Virginia A. *Children and Libraries: Getting It Right.* Chicago: American Library Association, 2001.

Whitmire, Richard. "Boy Trouble." *New Republic,* January 23, 2006, 15–18.

Wilhelm, Jeffrey D., and Michael Smith. "Asking the Right Questions: Literate Lives of Boys." *Reading Teacher,* May 2005, 788–89.

Williams, Bronwyn T. "Girl Power in a Digital World: Considering the Complexity of Gender, Literacy, and Technology." *Journal of Adolescent and Adult Literacy,* December 2006/January 2007, 300–307.

Wynne-Jones, Tim. "Short Tempered." *Horn Book,* May/June 1999, 293–300.

Young, Josephine Peyton, and William G. Brozo. "Boys Will Be Boys, or Will They? Literacy and Masculinities." *Reading Research Quarterly,* July/August/ September 2001, 316–25.

Index

You may also be interested in

Connecting Boys with Books: In this hit book, Sullivan provides the tools that librarians, school library media specialists, and educators need to overcome the cultural and developmental challenges, stereotyping, and lack of role models that essentially program boys out of the library. From playing chess to swathing the walls in butcher paper to give boys a physical space in which to respond to books, Sullivan's practical ideas and developmentally astute insights show librarian and teacher colleagues how to make vitally needed connections with this underserved population.

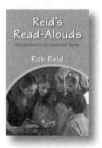

Fundamentals of Children's Services: Sullivan conducts a friendly tour in this comprehensive reference, covering both innovative and standard practices in children's services. From collection and programming, to homework support, reference, and reader's advisory, to promoting and budgeting, children's services parallel other library services in many ways. Part of ALA's Fundamentals Series, this overview provides hands-on, proven strategies for those on the front lines, while addressing questions critical to the long-term success of children's library services.

Reid's Read-Alouds: In this timesaving resource, Rob Reid makes reading aloud to children and teens easy by selecting titles in high-interest topics and providing context to spotlight great passages. Make reading fun and exciting with passages from 400 titles encompassing fiction and nonfiction, advice on how to prepare for a read-aloud, a subject index to make program planning easier, bibliographic information on all titles, and much more. You will find plenty to engage your audiences and reinvigorate programs!

Multicultural Programs for Tweens and Teens: This one-stop resource will help you encourage children and young adults to explore different cultures. The fifty flexible programming ideas allow you to choose a program specific to your scheduling needs; create an event that reflects a specific culture; and recommend further resources to tweens and teens interested in learning more about diverse cultures.

For more information, please visit www.alastore.ala.org.